An Introduction to Global Supply Chain Management, Second Edition

An Introduction to Global Supply Chain Management, Second Edition

What Every Manager Needs to Understand

Edmund Prater and Kim Whitehead

BEP

BUSINESS EXPERT PRESS

Leader in applied, concise business books

An Introduction to Global Supply Chain Management:
What Every Manager Needs to Understand, Second Edition

Copyright © Business Expert Press, LLC, 2023.

Cover design by Charlene Kronstedt

Interior design by Exeter Premedia Services Private Ltd., Chennai, India

First published in 2013 by
Business Expert Press, LLC
222 East 46th Street, New York, NY 10017
www.businessexpertpress.com

ISBN-13: 978-1-63742-455-1 (paperback)
ISBN-13: 978-1-63742-456-8 (e-book)

Business Expert Press Supply and Operations Management Collection

Second edition: 2023

10 9 8 7 6 5 4 3 2 1

Description

The problems during COVID made everyone aware that today's global business environment relies on supply chains 24/7.

Although most people are not supply chain experts, they *must* know and understand the key aspects of supply chain management to make the best daily decisions for their business. Many textbooks cover numerous details and theories about supply chains. However, it has been said that everything that is taught in business school is **theory** ... until you must make payroll.

Both authors have made payroll in various businesses. Thus, this text removes the details and is focused on an executive overview of the key aspects of global supply chains that every businessperson needs to know to continually **succeed in their business and make payroll**.

In order to succeed today you must speak different languages. This doesn't necessarily mean Chinese, German, or English. Rather it refers to the need to speak accounting, finance, marketing, and operations. This book is written for the executive who is not a supply chain management (SCM) professional but who wants to learn more about his or her supply chain. We will do this by diving into some best practices, examples of how other companies have managed their supply chain, and getting an overall briefing on the state of the art in SCM today. Questions and topics will be brought up, which will help you have an informed discussion with the SCM professionals in your company. As prior supply chain and manufacturing executives and now educators, we hope to share with you a mix of our professional and academic experience and knowledge that will provide you a framework for understanding the placement of your supply chain within the global marketplace.

Keywords

global supply chain management; value chain perspective; forecasting; logistics; distribution; inventory management; supply chain uncertainty; chaos management; supply chain coping strategies; information technology in supply chains; customer service within supply chains

Contents

CHAPTER 1

Supply Chain Management

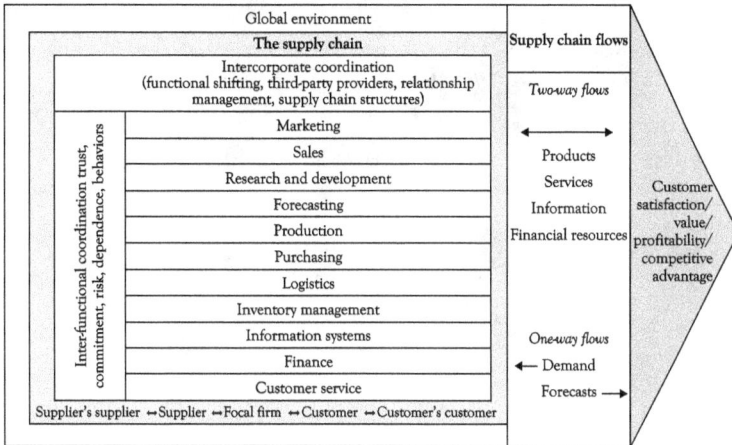

The diagram shows "Global environment" containing "The supply chain" and "Supply chain flows."

Within "The supply chain":
- Intercorporate coordination (functional shifting, third-party providers, relationship management, supply chain structures)
- Marketing
- Sales
- Research and development
- Forecasting
- Production
- Purchasing
- Logistics
- Inventory management
- Information systems
- Finance
- Customer service

Vertical label: Interfunctional coordination trust, commitment, risk, dependence, behaviors

Bottom row: Supplier's supplier ↔ Supplier ↔ Focal firm ↔ Customer ↔ Customer's customer

Supply chain flows:
- Two-way flows: Products, Services, Information, Financial resources
- One-way flows: ← Demand, Forecasts →
- Customer satisfaction/value/profitability/competitive advantage

Chapter Objectives

- Define terminology
- Introduce the concept of "supply chain management"
- Explore the pillars that support excellent supply chain management (SCM)
- Lay the foundation for the introduction of supply chain strategy

It is impossible to carry on a discussion of the current business environment without the term "supply chain" coming up. Warren Hausman of Stanford University sums it up well when he states that "Today's competition is not really company vs. company but supply chain vs. supply chain." Yet, what do we mean when we say, "supply chain" and what is required to manage one?

Cost

Speed

Flexibility

Dependability

Quality

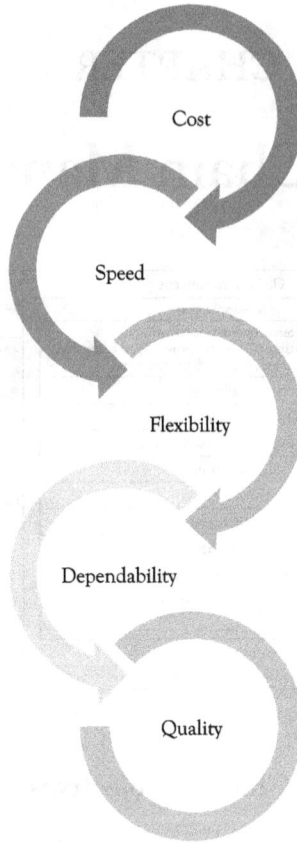

History of Supply Chain Management

Jay Forrester was considered the first person in academic literature to introduce the mindset of what is considered the supply chain view, in his seminal paper published in the *Harvard Business Review*.[1] The term *supply chain management* was first used by two consultants by the names of Oliver and Webber in 1982. However, this term did not just magically come into being. Instead, Oliver and Webber had a good view of the future because they were standing on the shoulders of the Japanese and the just-in-time (JIT) revolution of the 1970s. In order to get a better understanding of what constitutes a supply chain, consider the role of traditional performance indicators and how they function within business processes. Each is singularly important, but yet, each is dependent on one another within an interdependent system.

Given this reality, how should we respond and manage them?

The Japanese responded with a process known as JIT inventory controls. The goal of JIT is to produce products at the right time, at the right quantity, and with perfect quality. Likewise, the goal of SCM is at the right product, at the right time, at the right place, at a competitive price. Continuing this idea, in migrating from JIT to SCM, the following views must change:

- From flow-oriented to interfaces structure-oriented;
- From plant-oriented to relationship-oriented;
- From production-oriented to customer service-oriented.

But How Do You Make This Change?

SCM is concerned with the relationship between a company and its upstream and downstream partners; building relationships helps companies coordinate (work jointly) with their trading partners to integrate activities along the supply chain, to supply its customers with products effectively.

Who are these partners? As can be seen in **Phase 1** of Figure 1.1, a supply chain consists of a company and its suppliers and customers. This can be extended. Your immediate customer may have other customers of its own, while your supplier may have other subsuppliers. This general structure can be extended to include five general categories.

Producer

This is the company that either manufactures some product (such as a lawnmower) or provides some service (such as a lawn-mowing company).

Distributor

Purchases bulk quantities of manufactured goods from the producer and sells to other companies in large quantities—much larger than individuals would purchase—also known as a wholesaler.

Phase 1:
Independent
supply-chain
entities

Suppliers   Purchasing   Production   Distribution   Customers

Phase 2:
Internal
integration

Suppliers   Purchasing Production Distribution   Customers

Internal supply chain
materials management department

Phase 3:
Supply-chain
integration

Suppliers   Internal supply chain   Customers

Integrated supply chain

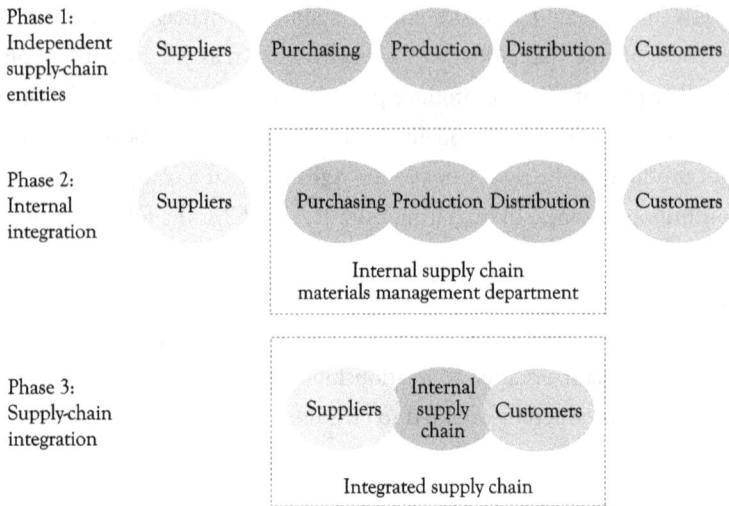

Figure 1.1 Supply chain relationships

Customer

A customer may be an individual who buys a product for personal use of an organization that buys products to be used to build other products of their own manufacture.

Service Provider

There are a host of providers of services in areas such as logistics, finance, HR management, IT support, marketing, design, and the list goes on.

In **Phase 2,** a firm begins to realize that instead of treating each part of the supply chain as a separate entity, it should begin to integrate functions. This allows firms to look for solutions that are best for the company as a whole, not just what's best for each individual department.

In **Phase 3,** a firm expands its viewpoint to incorporate all its upstream and downstream partners. This integrated supply chain is the long-term goal of SCM; however, you are limited by your supply chain's ability to *coordinate* activities and *integrate* different departments and companies; these two issues have different demands and structures. Specifically,

- **Integration**
  how closely supply chain entities operate as a single unit—focus on interfaces (structure). This is a static process.

- **Coordination**
  how seamlessly information, material and financial flows flow in
  the supply chain—focus on movement (process). This is a dynamic
  process.

The interaction of these two concepts defines the key relationship in
supply chains.

Without strong coordination and integration your company may
have:

- **Inaccurate forecasts**
  When each organization produces forecasts independent of each
  other, you increase the uncertainty in the system. This can result
  in the bullwhip effect (Figure 1.2) that we saw in the Beer Game,
  which we will discuss later in the course.
- Low-capacity **utilization**
  If you forecast a large demand and purchase equipment to produce
  that quantity, what happens if the demand isn't as large as forecasted?
  You have a lot of money tied up in machines that aren't being used.
- **Excess inventory**
  If you have produced a large amount of product in anticipation of
  high sales and those forecasted sales do not materialize, you have a
  lot of money tied up in these "extra" products and the cost to store
  them. In addition, you may be paying interest on the money you
  used to produce this excess inventory.
- **Obsolete inventory**
  If you have large amounts of excess inventory, these items tend
  to become obsolete over a period of time. This means that the

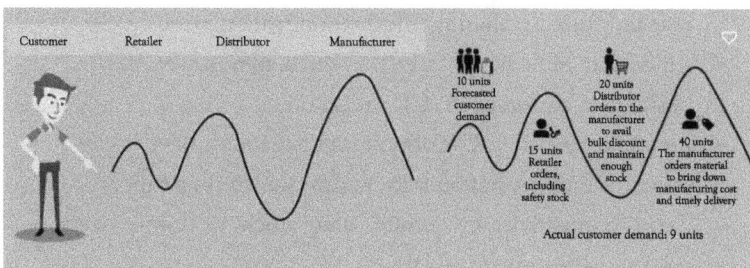

Figure 1.2 The Bullwhip effect

inventory can become outdated and/or no longer desired by your customer.

- **Inadequate customer service**
  If your forecast is too low, then you won't have products available when customers want to purchase them. This can result in lost sales and decreased market share.

All of these problems stemming from weak coordination and low integration can cause substantial difficulties for your company, both to your company's reputation and financial stability.

Focusing on *integration*, there are several key issues that must be addressed to make all the individual groups and companies in a supply chain operate in unison. They include:

- Choice of partners: Costs, future potential, organizational culture, specialized know-how, taxes, exchange rates, and so on.
- Interorganizational networking: Independent versus dependent; secret versus information/know-how sharing; long-term versus short-term; win–win strategy versus maximizing own profits, and so on.
- Leadership: At least some decisions should be made for the supply chain as a whole. Aligning strategies along the supply chain requires some form of leadership.

Likewise, *coordination* also has three key issues to consider. These issues allow groups in the supply chain to share information about current operations and future decisions.

- Utilization of Information Technology (IT): Historical data, demand forecast, sharing information instantaneously, electronic data interchange (EDI), business to business (B2B), business to customer (B2C), and so on.
- Process orientation: Use of performance indicators to determine weaknesses, bottlenecks, and waste within a supply chain (productivity, cycle time, safety stock, work-in-process, return-on-investment (ROI), etc.).

- Advanced planning: Incorporates long-term, mid-term, and short-term planning levels.

In essence, *coordination* and *integration* provide the framework for you to build your company's supply chain "house" (see the following House Diagram). Other management topics provide the foundation. Thus to support your SCM "house," you and/or your team should have relevant knowledge in:

- Logistics and transportation
- Marketing
- Operations management and research
- Organizational behavior, industrial organization, and transaction cost economics
- Cost accounting
- Purchasing and material management

When you incorporate these topics, you have the following housing framework (Figure 1.3).

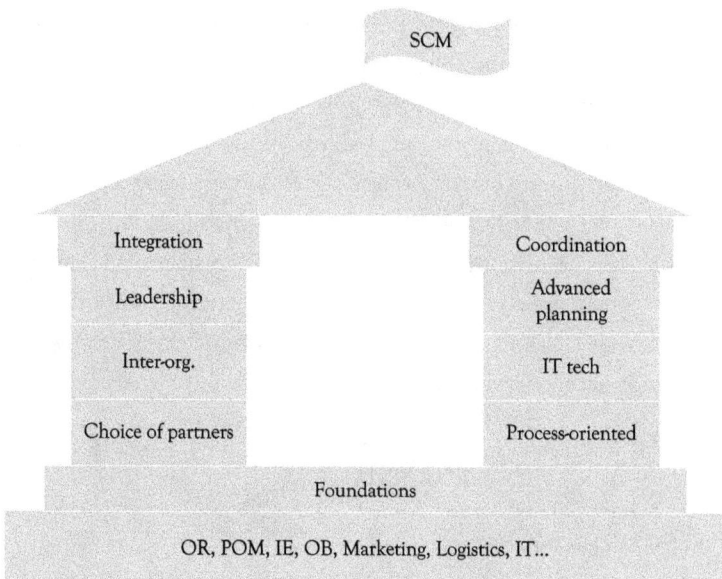

Figure 1.3 Supply chain management framework

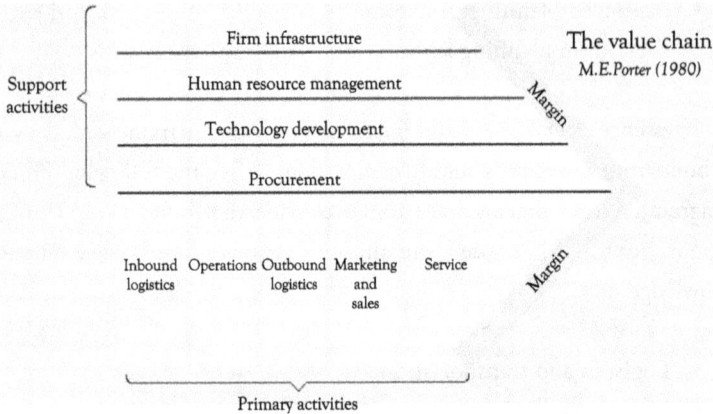

Figure 1.4 The value chain M.E. Porter (1980)

Another way of looking at this is to view it as a value chain issue. Michael Porter, in his classic book *Competitive Advantage* (New York: Free Press, 1980), developed the concept of the value chain in which a company is divided between primary and secondary, or support, activities. Primary value chain activities are those that are directly involved with producing a product for sale and delivering it to the customer. They culminate in the total value delivered by an organization. The "margin" depicted in the following Figure 1.4 is the same as added value. (All of the following is adapted from *Competitive Advantage*.)

Thus, we see that viewing the supply chain as a value chain activity provides us with basically the same viewpoint as the "house" of SCM. Whichever viewpoint you take, your chain is only as strong as its weakest link. Or, if you prefer the house analogy, if your foundations are weak, the house will fall. The major focus of SCM is on primary value chain activities. Secondary activities such as IT, while extremely important, are support activities. Thus, for the sake of this introductory course, we will not focus on secondary activities.

Key Takeaways

- SCM calls for changes:
  - From flow-oriented to interfaces-oriented;
  - From plant-oriented to relationship-oriented;
  - From production-oriented to customer service-oriented.

- Relationships are the key to SCM.
- Integration and coordination are the pillars of successful SCM.
- The focus of SCM is on the primary activities of the firm.

Reflection Points

1. A good starting point for considering how this applies to your company is to ask yourself about the relationships your company has with its upstream and downstream trading partners.
   - Are they friendly?
   - Hostile?
   - Long-term?
   - Short-term?
   - Competitive?
   - Win–Win?
2. Does your firm have an integrated view of SCM or does each department fend for itself?
3. What is the history of your company? How do you think its history has impacted the way its supply chain system has evolved?

Additional Resources

Cottrill, K. 1997. "Reforging the Supply Chain." *Journal of Business Strategy* 18, no. 6, pp. 35–39.

Davis, T. Summer 1993. "Effective Supply Chain Management." *Sloan Management Review,* pp. 35–46.

Fawcett, S.F. and G.M. Magnan. 2002. "The Rhetoric and Reality of Supply Chain Integration." *International Journal of Physical Distribution and Logistics Management 32,* no. 5, pp. 339–361.

Fisher, M.L. 1997. "What Is the Right Supply Chain for Your Product?" *Harvard Business Review* 75, no. 2, pp. 105–117.

Mangan, J. and C. Lalwani. 2016. *Global Logistics and Supply Chain Management,* 3rd ed, pp. 1–2. John Wiley & Sons.

Mintzberg, H. 1994. "Rethinking Strategic Planning Part I: Pitfalls and Fallacies." *Long Range Planning 27,* no. 3, pp. 12–21.

Stock, G.N., N.P. Greis, and J.D. Kasarda. 2000. "Enterprise Logistics and Supply Chain Structure: The Role of Fit." *Journal of Operations Management* 18, pp. 531–547.

The M. Conley Company. n.d. *Bullwhip Effect.* [image]. www.mconley.com/assets/images/home/blog/bullwhip.png.

Multiple Choice Questions

1. Who was first noted for using the term *supply chain management* in 1982?

    a. W. Edwards Deming

    b. Oliver and Webber

    c. Jay Forrester

    d. Taiichi Ohno

    e. Joseph Juran

2. Supply chain management (SCM) focuses on all the following activities except:

    a. Logistics

    b. Customer service

    c. Human Resources

    d. Marketing

    e. Scheduling production

3. The sourcing and receiving of raw materials for subsequent use is best described as:

    a. Physical distribution

    b. Materials management

    c. Material flow system

    d. Supply chain management

    e. Inventory management

4. Supply chain management focuses on business _____ and their integration.

    a. Functions

    b. Departments

    c. Relationships

    d. Processes

    e. Advantages

5. A(n) _____ supply chain is concerned with its relationships with upstream and downstream partners in addition to its internal supply chain.

  a. Logistics
  b. Integrated
  c. Reverse
  d. Independent
  e. Dependent

6. What is not a problem when there is weak coordination and integration between companies in a supply chain?

  a. High capacity utilization
  b. Inaccurate forecasts
  c. Excess inventory
  d. Inadequate customer service
  e. Obsolete inventory

7. Which of the following is not a key issue that coordination considers?

  a. Process orientation
  b. Advance planning
  c. Utilization of Information Technology
  d. Choice of partners

8. _____ activities are those that are directly involved with producing a product for sale and delivering it.

  a. Coordination
  b. Integration
  c. Secondary value chain
  d. Primary value chain
  e. Distribution

9. Which of the following best describes a distributor?

  a. Company that either manufacturers some product or provides some service.

    b. Company that purchases bulk quantities of manufactured goods and sells to other companies in large quantities.

    c. Individual who buys a product for personal use or an organization that buys products for resale or to be used in other products.

    d. Company that provides services in areas such as logistics, finance, human resource management, and so on.

    e. Company that buys a product and ships directly to the end consumer from the seller.

10. What management style did supply chain management evolve from?

    a. Human resource management

    b. Value chain management

    c. Logistics management

    d. Competitive advantage

    e. Just-in-time

11. _____ is the individual who buys a product for personal use or an organization that buys products to be resold or used to build other products of their own manufacture.

    a. Producer

    b. Distributor

    c. Customer

    d. Service provider

    e. Coordinator

12. According to Feargal Quinn, "Genuine _____ ability is one of the few true forms of competitive advantage."

    a. Management

    b. Leadership

    c. Listening

    d. Marketing

    e. Friendliness

13. Who in his book, *Competitive Advantage*, developed the concept of the value chain?

    a. Jay Forrester
    b. Michael Porter
    c. Oliver and Webber
    d. Joseph Juran
    e. Walter Shewhart

14. Logistics activities include all the following except:

    a. Forecasting demand
    b. Inventory management
    c. Return approval and acceptance
    d. Product design
    e. Delivery to a customer

15. What is the *major focus* of supply chain management?

    a. Value chain activities
    b. Information Technology
    c. Coordination and integration
    d. Forecasting demand
    e. Management of the storage and flow of goods, services, and information.

CHAPTER 2

The Global Stage

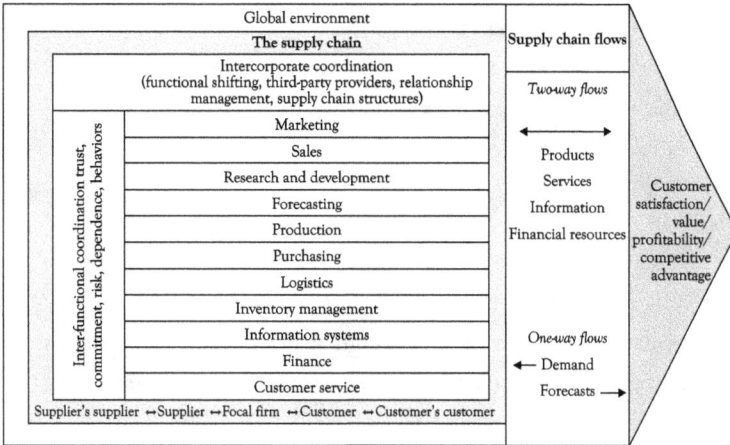

		Global environment		
		The supply chain	Supply chain flows	
		Intercorporate coordination (functional shifting, third-party providers, relationship management, supply chain structures)	Two-way flows	
Inter-functional coordination trust, commitment, risk, dependence, behaviors		Marketing		
		Sales	Products	
		Research and development	Services	Customer satisfaction/ value/ profitability/ competitive advantage
		Forecasting	Information	
		Production	Financial resources	
		Purchasing		
		Logistics		
		Inventory management		
		Information systems	One-way flows	
		Finance	Demand	
		Customer service	Forecasts	
Supplier's supplier ↔ Supplier ↔ Focal firm ↔ Customer ↔ Customer's customer				

Chapter Objectives

- Introduce the types of global supply chains
- Explore the forces that affect the global economy
- Discuss the consequences of foreign markets
- Consider supply chain global strategies

Supply Chains in the Global Marketplace

International and global are words that tend to be used interchangeably when it comes to global supply chain and logistics. However, the two terms represent two different scenarios, resulting in an inaccurate depiction when grouping them together. *International* involves two or more nations, while *global* refers to influencing the entire world. Before we discuss globalization, we need to have a basis for discussion. Different

types of firms exist and compete in the global marketplace. We distin-
guish them, at a high level, in the following ways:

Multinational Firm

- Majority ownership in either foreign sales organization/distri-
  bution networks or production plants.
- Active in more than one country.
- May have a borderless global culture and tailor production
  and markets to local needs such as Proctor & Gamble and
  McDonalds.

Global Firm

- Coordinated production, sales, distribution, and administra-
  tive networks that focus on singular products that do not have
  to be adapted to a large degree for individual markets such as
  Coke, Walt Disney, and Sony.

Domestic Firm

- All others.

Within each of these types of firms, it is no surprise to practitioners of
SCM that daily supply chain decisions are impacted by global forces. To
better understand this impact, companies in general and SCM managers
in particular need to ask three main questions that will drive the rest of
our discussion:

1. What are the forces shaping the global economy?
2. What are the consequences of globalization?
3. How can we take advantage of the dynamic globalization process?

What Are the Forces That Shape the Global Economy?

1. Global market forces
2. Technological forces

3. Global cost forces

4. Political and macroeconomic forces

Global Market Forces

These forces tend to be the issues that are immediately seen from a competitive perspective. For example, there is increased foreign competition, which makes it more difficult to compete in the local market. A classic example is the growth of competition in the automotive market. In the 1960s, the U.S. market generally consisted of the Big Firms: AMC, Mercedes, BMW, Porsche, and Jaguar. Contrast that to the worldwide auto market of the present day. The increase in global markets has led to shorter product lives, more customization, and faster response to market demands. For example, automobile manufacturers now come out with a new model in less than 4 years, whereas before they worked in 10-year cycles. There are key implications to this decrease in product lives, namely:

- Traditional product life-cycle approach to international production is no longer valid.
- Simultaneous product development is needed in all markets.
- Local presence and representation needed for customization and fast response.

The product life-cycle approach first took the view that companies would introduce a product in their home market. After the new introduction phase, the product moved toward high-volume production. As the product matured and low cost became a major factor, production was moved offshore to decrease costs while the products would also begin to be sold to overseas markets. That model no longer holds. Today, simultaneous product development and release is necessary in all worldwide markets. In addition, a local presence is needed in all worldwide markets to allow for firms to customize their products to that particular marketplace and respond quickly to any market changes.

Technological Forces

All of you are taking this course online, not through a correspondence program based on paper. This illustrates one of the major technical impacts of our time, the Web. Next, notice the global issues involved in using the Web. HTML was developed by a British researcher. The first browser, Mosaic, was developed by a U.S. graduate student. The structure of the network was developed by U.S. defense researchers (excluding Al Gore) and you are probably accessing the Web using computers with parts manufactured in Japan and Southeast Asia.

A presence in state-of-the-art markets is useful to a company for maintaining its technological edge. Examples of state-of-the-art markets include:

Japan: Semiconductor process equipment, consumer electronics, machine tools
Germany: Machine tools
Scandinavia: Cellular phones, wireless products and services
United States: Aerospace, computers, software

Production facilities in these state-of-the-art markets also serve as market sensors, which allow supply chains to have advanced notice of changes in the marketplace. They also serve as learning laboratories to try out new technologies and services.

Global Cost Forces

Increased global competition has driven down costs. To use the automotive market as an example again, there has been a 20-year decrease in costs on automotive technology, parts, and vehicles. This has been driven by the fact that many growing countries help subsidize the growth of heavy industrial production firms such as those in the automotive industry in an effort to expand local jobs. This has led to a worldwide glut of production capacity driving down costs. Another issue that is currently a major concern to employees is the topic of offshore outsourcing. Many firms are moving jobs overseas where labor costs are lower. However, overall, within the worldwide business community, there has been a shift away from offshore strategies driven solely by a low labor cost mentality. This is because of the diminishing importance of direct labor cost in the production of many products. This in turn has led to a reduction in the

"Island Hopping" syndrome where firms have moved from producing in Japan to Singapore, Hong Kong, Malaysia, China, and so on, in search of lowest labor costs. Instead, new competitive priorities are driving global location. These include priorities such as

- Access to markets
- Access to skilled workers
- Quality
- Availability of suppliers
- Reliability of suppliers
- Transport time and costs

Political and Macroeconomic Forces

Because of the increase in free trade and the reduction of tariff barriers, there is an increase in competition. Likewise, there has been an increase in global trade groups. These include:

- APEC (Pacific countries)
- EU (Europe)
- MERCOSUR (South America)
- NAFTA (North America)
- SEATO (Australia, New Zealand, Japan, Hong Kong, South Korea, Chile)

In addition, the development of regional free-trade groups force companies to rethink regional production strategies; examples include the EU and NAFTA. While these trade organizations and GATT have been successful in reducing official trade barriers, countries still impose nontariff barriers that favor the globalization of production strategies and their attendant supply chains. These nontariff barriers include, but are not limited to:

- Voluntary export restraints (U.S.–Japan: autos);
- Trigger price mechanisms (U.S. semiconductor and steel industry);

- Local content requirement (European auto and semiconductor industry);
- Technical standards and health regulations;
- Government procurement policies.

What Are the Consequences of Globalization?

In general, the consequences of globalization on supply chains can be grouped into three areas:

- Increasing cooperation among logistics and operations areas of different members of the supply chain.
- Functional integration both internally and with joint ventures.
- Search for improved geographical integration including knowledge, technology, raw materials, and so on.

Increasing Cooperation Among Logistics and Operations Areas

This topic will be dealt with more in-depth in a future segment. However, one international indication of this trend is the growth of global third-party logistics providers. These firms help integrate logistics, operations, and other supply chain functions. This is done not just by providing basic logistics functions but by also offering logistics information systems and enterprise resource planning (ERP) capabilities to integrate in other supply chain functions of the firm they are providing services to.

Integration of Internal Functions Both Internally and With Joint Ventures

To provide a global example of the first issue, one can look at technology-driven joint ventures. Within the automotive market there are joint ventures between General Motors–Toyota, Chrysler–Mitsubishi, and Ford–Mazda. All these are focused at streamlining technology and product development and reducing costs. Another reason for global integration is the increasing capital intensity of production facilities. For example,

Semiconductor plants

- 1986: 50M$–100M$
- 1994: 250M$–400M$ (R&D over 1B$)
- 2004: 1B$+

By pursuing these integrated joint ventures, manufacturers share costs and risks. Several firms such as Texas Instruments and Hitachi, Motorola and Toshiba, and IBM and Siemens shared production facilities for DRAM chips.

Search for Improved Geographical Integration

The following are examples of the need for global locations to access critical components.

- Canon (controls 80 percent of engines for fax machines and laser printers).
- Fanuc (machine tool controllers).

Global locations also allow access to process technology. Examples here include U.S. Semiconductor manufacturers in Japan for access to photolithography technology and IBM & Xerox in Japan for access to video technology.

Key Takeaways

- Every organization is affected by globalization in one way or another. Managers should be aware of the factors that drive globalization affects such as:
  - º Global market forces
  - º Technological forces
  - º Global cost forces
  - º Political and macroeconomic forces
- These forces should be addressed proactively and a part of every overarching business strategy.

- Again, we see the importance of integration and coordination within the supply chain. The best-laid plans for ensuring integration and coordination still fail when they do not ensure that the implemented processes are maintained and audit them from time to time to ensure that the processes are still serving the needs of the organization.

Reflection Points

1. What have been the impacts of the global marketplace on your company?
2. What are the current global market forces that your firm has to respond to?
3. What impacts does your company make on the global economy?

Additional Resources

Bovet, D. January/February 2004. "Europe's New Growth Driver: The Supply Chain Can Open the Door to Higher Profits and More Streamlined Operations for Companies Operating in Europe." *Supply Chain Management Review*, pp. 9–17.

Mangan, J. and C. Lalwani. 2016. *Global Logistics and Supply Chain Management*, 3rd ed., pp. 13–14. John Wiley & Sons.

Mangan, J. and C. Lalwani. 2016. *Global Logistics and Supply Chain Management*, 3rd ed., pp. 24–25. John Wiley & Sons.

Omar, A., B. Davis-Sramek, M. Myers, and J. Mentzer. 2012. "A Global Analysis of Orientation, Coordination and Flexibility in Supply Chains." *Journal of Business Logistics* 33, no. 2, pp. 128–144.

Yip, G.S. September 1982. "Gateways to Entry." *Harvard Business Review*, pp. 85–91.

Multiple Choice Questions

1. What best describes a firm that is active in more than one country and has high local responsiveness in their products and marketing?

   a. Global firm
   b. International firm
   c. Multinational firm

    d. Domestic firm

    e. Transnational firm

2. What is not one of the forces that shape the global economy?

    a. Market forces

    b. Technological forces

    c. Global Cost forces

    d. Domestic forces

    e. Political and macroeconomic forces

3. The increase in global market competition has led to all of the following except:

    a. Shorter product lives

    b. More customization

    c. Faster response to market demands

    d. Simultaneous product development and releases

    e. Introduction of new products to a company's home market first

4. Which country specializes in semiconductor process equipment?

    a. Korea

    b. United States

    c. Japan

    d. Germany

    e. China

5. Which of the following is an example of a political/macroeconomic force?

    a. General agreements of tariffs and trade

    b. Availability of suppliers

    c. Proximity to raw materials

    d. Decrease in product life cycles

    e. Transport time and costs

6. Which of the following is not an example of global cost forces?

    a. Access to markets

    b. Trigger price mechanisms

    c. Access to skilled workers

    d. Reliability of suppliers

    e. Reduced labor costs

7. What best describes operations granted to a licensee in exchange for a lump sum payment, per unit royalty fee, or a proportion of profits?

    a. Joint venture

    b. Wholly owned subsidiary

    c. Franchising

    d. Exporting

    e. Management contract

8. Managers should address global forces that drive globalization _____.

    a. Simultaneously

    b. Reactively

    c. Through strategic alliances

    d. Proactively

    e. Through joint ventures

9. When the firm chooses an entry option that does not include a foreign partner it is considered a _____.

    a. Strategic alliance

    b. Local content requirement

    c. Domestic firm

    d. Stand-alone entry

10. Which of the following is not one of the global trade groups discussed in this chapter?

    a. European Union—EU

    b. Asia-Pacific Economic Cooperation—APEC

    c. North America Free Trade Agreement—NAFTA

    d. Association of South East Asian Nations—ASEAN

11. What best describes and ownership split agreement?

    a. Exporting

    b. Joint venture

    c. Wholly owned subsidiary

    d. Licensing

    e. Franchising

12. What best describes when manufacturers share costs and risks to streamline technology and product development?

    a. Integration of internal functions with joint ventures

    b. Market forces

    c. Increased cooperation among logistics and operations areas

    d. Technological forces

    e. Improved geographical integration

13. Which type of firm has a presence in more than one country but whose product are unchanged across multiple cultures?

    a. Domestic firm

    b. Multinational firm

    c. Global firm

    d. Transnational firm

    e. Multidomestic firm

14. Operations granted to the licensee in exchange for a lump sum payment, per unit royalty fee or proportion of the profits is considered a

    a. Licensing option

    b. Wholly owned subsidiary option

    c. Exporting option

    d. Joint venture option

15. When a firm chooses an entry option that does not include a foreign partner; it is considered a _____ entry.

    a. Franchise

    b. Stand-alone

    c. SEATO

    d. APEC

CHAPTER 3

Forecasting

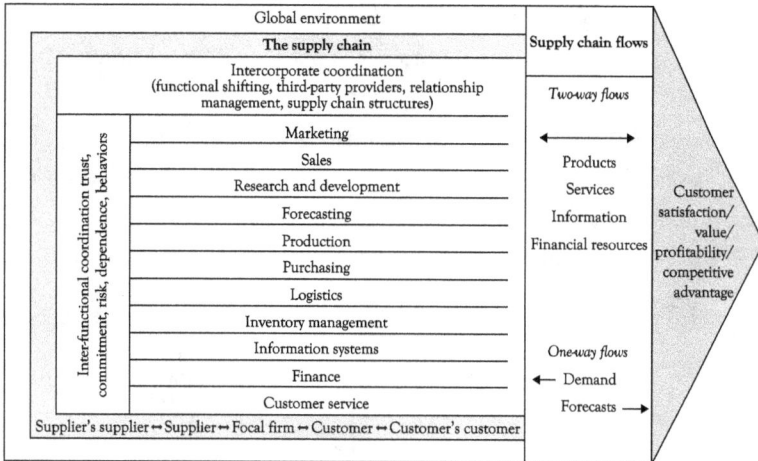

Global environment		
The supply chain	Supply chain flows	
Intercorporate coordination (functional shifting, third-party providers, relationship management, supply chain structures)	Two-way flows	
Marketing	⟵⟶	
Sales	Products	
Research and development	Services	Customer satisfaction/ value/ profitability/ competitive advantage
Forecasting	Information	
Production	Financial resources	
Purchasing		
Logistics		
Inventory management		
Information systems	One-way flows	
Finance	⟵ Demand	
Customer service	Forecasts ⟶	
Supplier's supplier ↔ Supplier ↔ Focal firm ↔ Customer ↔ Customer's customer		

(Left vertical label: Inter-functional coordination trust, commitment, risk, dependence, behaviors)

Chapter Objectives

- Introduce forecasting methods;
- Explore the facets of forecasts and their dynamic nature;
- Discuss how forecasts can be optimized;
- Explore types of future outlooks;
- Considering forecasting best practices;
- Apply forecasting in a mini-case.

In order to survive in today's competitive markets, the forecasting process must be mastered. We introduce you to the five viewpoints a forecaster can have of the future and describe particularities in international forecasting. In addition, this chapter shows benchmarks in the forecasting process, the models used, and the applied software solutions and systems. Finally, a best practice solution is presented, and emergent phenomena are introduced that show the trend for forecasting in the future.

Forecasting Methods

There are four basic forecasting methodologies defined by Chopra and Meindl at Northwestern (Chopra and Meindl 2004):

Qualitative: Forecasting based on personal insight or intuition.

Causal: This assumes that specific variables drive the forecast. For example, interest rate increases by the Fed may decrease commercial loan activity. Or, your customer is opening 25 new stores, which will increase your sales to that customer.

Time series: Assumes that historical data will predict future trends. For example, some companies forecast sales each month based on the sales at the same time last year.

Simulation: Combines causal and time series methods in order to try out what-if scenarios.

Most companies use a combination of these techniques to create their forecasts.

Key Concepts in Forecasting

Forecasting is more accurate for short timeframes than when used for long-term planning. For example, when Walmart had their stores begin ordering every two weeks rather than each month, inventories were reduced because forecasting accuracy increased. This most likely resulted in an increase in their purchasing and ordering costs; however, the benefits of reducing inventory and safety stock outweighs the increased ordering costs.

Different forecasting tools are applicable for different applications and timeframes. The following table (Table 3.1) provides a basic comparison of the types of forecasts routinely done by organizations.

Additionally, there are five concepts that must always be taken into account when planning for the future. These are as follows:

- *Impact of Technology:* If, in the 1970s, you were the CEO of Smith Corona typewriters and had not considered the impact of PCs on your business, you would have been blown out of

Table 3.1 *Forecasting Timeframe Application*

Application	Short Term (0–3 mo.)	Medium Term (3 mo. to 2 yr.)	Long Term (more than 2 yr.)
Forecast Quantity	Individual products or services	Total sales groups or families of products or services	Total sales
Decision Area	Inventory management, final assembly scheduling, workforce scheduling, master production scheduling	Staff planning, production planning, master production scheduling, purchasing distribution	Facility location, capacity planning, process management
Forecasting Technique	Time series, causal, qualitative	Time series, causal, qualitative	Causal, qualitative, simulation

the water (which is exactly what happened). The same could be said about filmmakers and companies creating mp3 players or CDs, which are all built into one in this day and age with smartphones.

- *Social Issues*: For example, microwave ovens were available in the 1950s, but the market was not there since most women were not working outside the home.
- *Political Issues*: For example, when governments offer subsidies for the development of new products, this can cause accelerated product introduction. Hybrid vehicles in California are one such example.
- *Legal Issues*: The federal breakup of Bell Telephone significantly impacted the rate at which new products and services were offered by the phone company (companies).
- *Environmental Issues*: For example, the demand for cleaner air can drive the development of new technologies and services. On the other hand, wide-open spaces such as in Dallas, Texas, do not pressure the population to make use of services such as mass transit like citizens in Boston, MA, who are forced to take advantage of their mass transit system owing to the city's significant population density and limited space due to the adjacent harbor.

Given the importance of forecasting, it is often perplexing to see that companies have no centralized structure in place to ensure data capture and accuracy. Without appropriate and accurate data, forecasts are not reliable. Often, different divisions within the same company use different methods, software, and databases to forecast creating *isolated islands of information.*

Meanwhile, overall company forecasts are difficult to construct and have reduced accuracy because the various software packages and databases are not compatible. This is a classic example of what can happen when companies focus on business functions rather than business processes.

This is another case of not speaking the same language, which builds walls between functions, departments, and team members.

Breakthroughs in technology make it possible for companies to gather relevant information more readily than in the past. Yet, many companies are caught in the traditional **functionalist syndrome** *that continues to perpetuate departmental forecasts*—that are not fully integrated into an overall aggregate plan fitted to the prevailing corporate strategy.

Optimize Forecasting

To optimize the process of forecasting, business units have to:

- Collaborate with other units inside and partners outside the company.
- Have the capacity of a company to integrate its suppliers and customers into its forecasting processes.
- Be proactive in becoming involved in programs such as VMI (vendor-managed inventory) and CPFR (collaborative planning, forecasting, and replenishment).
- Assign accountability—and mean it!
- Ensure that all parties involved in forecasting are using the same "language" and understand each other's concerns, contributions, and expectations.

- Allow the forecast to be wrong—no one can predict the future 100 percent correctly. Don't let the fear of being wrong bog down the process.
- Continually improve the forecasting process—don't settle for *good enough*!

In the past, companies have mainly forecasted intuitively based on managerial insights, experience, and instincts. In recent years, however, companies favor scientific approaches that are based on facts and data. Each department has to forecast its business for the upcoming period to optimize the overall performance of the company. Technology enables the storage of large amounts of data in data warehouses. Forecasting software and processes apply models that can improve precision of forecasts.

Five Viewpoints of the Future

The viewpoints of supply chain managers determine the selection of forecasting information. It is imperative to backup forecasts with both logical and credible data, but credibility varies depending on the audience and situation. As a consequence, some thought should be given in determining what angle to seek when choosing forecasting methods, based on the decision maker's viewpoints of the future. There are five basic categories to which these viewpoints can be classified to help determine adequate forecasting methods. They are extrapolators, pattern analysts, goal analysts, counter-punchers, and intuitors. The key is to realize that neither viewpoint alone is perfect for every situation, but the right combination of these viewpoints and their techniques will produce the most valid information for supply chain managers.

Extrapolators

Extrapolators fall into the quantitative category when it comes to the type of data that they value in coming up with forecasts. Their basic belief is that the future is reasonably predictable, based on past trends. One

FIVE VIEW POINTS OF THE FUTURE				
Extrapolators	Pattern Analysts	Goal Analysts	Counter Punchers	Intuitors

• Technology
• Trend Analysis
 	
• Fisher-Pry
• Analysis
 	
• Gompertz
 	
• Growth Limit
• Analysis
 	
• Learning Curve
	• Analogy
	  Analysis
	
	• Precursor
	  Trend
	• Analysis
	
	• Morphological
	• Matrices
	
	• Feedback
	  Models
		• Impact Analysis
		
		• Content Analysis
		
		• Stakeholder
		  Analysis
		
		• Patent Analysis
		
		• Roadmaps
			• Scanning,
			• Monitoring,
			• Tracking
			
			• Alternate
			• Scenarios
			
			• Cross Impact
			• Analysis
				• Delphi Surveys
				
				• Nominal
				  Group
				• Conferencing
				
				• Structured
				• And Unstructured
				• Interviews
				
				• Competitor
				• Analysis

Quantitative ⟷ Qualitative

Forecasts

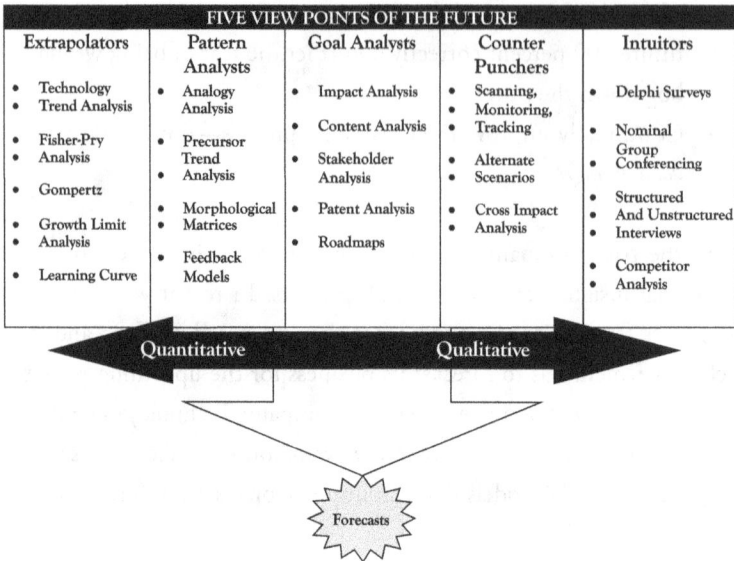

weakness of this belief is that it fails to take dramatic changes into consideration that could occur in the present but are not considered in the past data. Engineers usually follow this viewpoint on the future. Common techniques and methods used are as follows:

- Trend extrapolation: Where data sets are analyzed with an eye to identifying relevant trends that can be extended in time to predict capability.
- Fisher-Pry and Gompertz substitution analysis: Based on the observation that new technologies tend to follow a specific trend as they are deployed, developed, and reach maturity or market saturation. Gompertz and Fisher-Pry analyses are two techniques suited to fitting historical trend data to predict, among other things, when products are nearing maturity and likely to be replaced by new technology.
- Growth limit analysis.
- Learning curves.

Pattern Analysts

Pattern analysts also value quantitative information and are very similar to extrapolators. They basically believe that history repeats itself and that one may forecast the future by identifying and analyzing situations from the past and applying the cycles to future circumstances. A good example of a pattern analyst is a pure scientist. Common techniques and methods used are as follows:

- Analog analysis: Forecasting by analogy involves identifying past situations or technologies similar to the one of current interest and using historical data to project future developments. Research has shown that the accuracy of this forecasting technique can be improved by using a structured approach to identify the best analogies to use, wherein several possible analogies are identified and rated with respect to their relevance to the topic of interest.
- Precursor trend analysis.
- Morphological analysis: An understanding of how technologies evolve over time can be used to project future developments. It uses the laws of technological evolution, which describe how technologies change throughout their lifetimes because of innovation and other factors, leading to new products, applications, and technologies.
- Feedback models.

Goal Analysts

Goal analysts rely less on quantitative data and more on the belief that the future is determined by the actions and beliefs of a collection of individuals, organizations, and institutions. Their basis of forecasting is determining the goals of trendsetters and supply chain managers and figuring out how large an impact they can have on future trends. Individuals in marketing are usually goal analysts. This thinking not only takes on a more real-world approach but also does not emphasize the importance of other forces that impact change. Forecasting methods and techniques commonly used are as follows:

- Impact analysis
- Content analysis
- Stakeholder analysis
- Patent analysis

Counter-Punchers

Counter-punchers are on the qualitative side of the spectrum when it comes to the data that they use in forecasting. Their belief is that the future is a result of random events and the best way to stay in tune is to follow trends and plan accordingly. There is a high degree of judgment used in this type of forecast. Typical counter-punchers are usually executives. Common techniques and methods used are as follows:

- Scanning, monitoring, and tracking
- Alternate scenarios
- Cross-impact analysis

Intuitors

Finally, intuitors believe that a mixture of driving forces, random events, and the actions of key individuals and institutions shapes the future. The world is too complex to use a rational technique to project the future, so one should gather all the data available and use personal intuition to make forecasts. Intuitors are usually executives, as well. Their common techniques and methods are as follows:

- Delphi surveys: The Delphi method is a structured approach to eliciting forecasts from groups of experts, with an emphasis on producing an informed consensus view of the most probable future.
- Nominal group analysis.
- Structured and unstructured interviews.

Levels of Forecasting

Forecasting is one important part of company achievement. One must know the number of products the customers want. However, world trading is changing to a global supply and demand chain. Knowing local customers and doing organizational forecasting is not enough. Companies must carry on international forecasting, as well.

Organizational Forecasting

The main factors affecting accuracy at this level are the following:

- Sales and marketing involvement
- Software design procedures
- Forecasting team structure
- Data input
- Parameter setting
- Sales and operation planning

Top-Down Approach

This approach is common and simple because companies forecast on an aggregate level by using basic inputs such as historical data and promotion effects. It is suitable for predictable sales trends; however, management sometimes biases forecasting results because they are trying to meet sales targets.

Bottom-Up Approach

This approach is more complex than the first one. There is a larger number of forecasters involved. Sales representatives or local officers usually forecast at a local level. The approach is proper for specific promotional products and effective in planning for warehousing, manufacturing, and transportation. The disadvantage is that lower level historical data is usually lost or not completed.

International Level

All factors mentioned in the organizational level forecast still have an effect on forecasting results, but cultural differences among regions will be another important factor. For example, Latin American cultures prefer bright and vibrant colors, while Asians do not. Also, Americans prefer sweeter foods than Europeans do. Therefore, when companies engage in international forecasting, culture cannot be overlooked.

The Forecasting Process

Among the forecasting functions, people, process, technology, and resources, the process is the most important factor. It connects people to technology and resources. Because all departments of a company have to be involved in the forecasting process, it is essential to coordinate and synchronize actions among them. The lead-time determines how far ahead a forecast has to be conducted. The shorter the lead-time, the higher the probability of achieving accurate forecasts.

To take full advantage a company has to synchronize forecast-period and lead-time. To make the forecast as precise as possible, forecasted and actual results have to be monitored and compared carefully. In an ever-changing business environment, companies have to make sure that their forecasting process still meets market realities.

Best Practices in Forecasting

Forecasting is essential in any fast-moving sector where demand or product mix changes. Experience over the last few decades of commercial forecasting has identified good practices, which improve the likelihood of providing effective forecasting. A good forecast should be timely, accurate, reliable, made in meaningful units for the users, simple to understand, and documented in a way that enables later review.

For a Good Forecast...

- Focus on short-range forecasts as these are the drivers of immediate sales and replenishment activities.
- Forecast at a product family level wherever possible as this will be more accurate than the individual Stock Keeping Unit (SKU) level.
- The original forecasts should be retained and regularly measured for errors using various techniques.
- The forecaster should understand the business well to review and finalize the forecast.
- A good forecasting software should be used that will provide an easy to use and visual interface, as well as good forecasting tools.

Mini-Case

Why Supply Chain Forecasting Is a Best Practice at HP

When HP merged with Compaq, managers needed simple and consistent supply chain models for the combined businesses. They knew that they had to identify the best practices in each organization and apply them to the merged operations. The management used a wide range of communication techniques, supported by computing infrastructure, in order to find large savings for the combined operations. The parties agreed on common business tools and published their choice so that it was available for other members of the organization. At every node of the supply chain, a consensus forecast confronts net demand and supply. As a consequence, a detailed communication flow was provided for all members of the supply chain. The forecast of demand is updated on a daily basis. If a plan changes, the reason has to be explained to the supply chain partners. HP uses SAP's ERP software and uses the Internet to distribute a daily action plan, based on the demand forecast, to all the impacted members of the supply chain. HP's Inkjet division cut its forecasting time for the supply cycle by three days. The enterprise server group business unit has shortened the change order process from three weeks to just 24 hours. Through all their measures, HP continuously increased the efficiency of its operations and enhanced its customer satisfaction.

Key Takeaways

- In a dynamic and global marketplace, rules of the game change rapidly due to factors such as uncertainty in demand, changes in technology, and changes in competition.
- Business forecasters attempt to control the demand uncertainties by using various forecasting techniques also by using a fair amount of insights, judgment, and intuition.
- Forecasting may be done at the individual, organizational, and international levels.
  - At an individual level, customer tastes and preferences are considered.
  - The organizational level will include the aggregated data on consumers, advertising effects, and economic trends.

    ◦ Analysis at the international level may focus on cultural differences between countries in terms of power–distance, uncertainty avoidance, individualism/collectivism, and masculinity/femininity.

- Any business problem or opportunity requires valid forecasts, which should start with defining the objectives of the forecast.
- Various techniques may be selected from different views since the validity of the forecast will depend on the breadth of techniques used.
- Fight functionalist syndrome and watch the accuracy of your forecasts increase.

Reflection Points

1. Does your company have "functionalist syndrome?" If so, what can you and/or your team do to improve integration and cooperation using technology? What other methods could you use to improve forecasting in your company?
2. What approach does your company take to forecasting? Is the approach taken, the same one throughout the organization?
3. What type of quality control do you have in place to ensure that your forecasts are meeting the needs of the organization?
4. As a leader, do you understand the forecasting process in your company? Truly understand how it was developed, how it works, and if it is being changed to meet the needs of the organization as required?

Additional Resources

Dobosz, A. and A. Dougal. May/June 2012. "Releasing Supply Chain Value." *Supply Chain Solutions 42, no. 3,* pp. 72–74.

Lee, H. L. and C. Billington. September 1993. "Material Management in Decentralized Supply Chains." *Operations Research 41, no. 5,* pp. 835–847.

Muzumdar, M. and N. Balachandran. October 2001. "The Supply Chain Evolution: Roles, Responsibilities, and Implications for Management." *APICS the Performance Advantage.*

National Research Council; Division on Engineering and Physical Sciences; Committee on Forecasting Future Disruptive Technologies. 2010. *Persistent Forecasting of Disruptive Technologies.* The National Academies Press. www.nap.edu/read/12557/chapter/4 (retrieved March 13, 2021).

Multiple Choice Questions

1. Without _____ and _____ data, forecasts are not reliable.

   a. Timely; aggregated
   b. Centralized; aggregated
   c. Historical; centralized
   d. Appropriate; accurate
   e. Qualitative; time series

2. Which of the following forecast techniques is not typically used for long-term forecasting?

   a. Causal
   b. Qualitative
   c. Time series
   d. Simulation
   e. Delphi surveys

3. You have adopted the forecasting viewpoint of a pattern analyst. Which of the following is a technique that you would commonly use?

   a. Trend extrapolation
   b. Morphological analysis
   c. Delphi surveys
   d. Scanning, monitoring, and tracking
   e. Structured and unstructured interviews

4. Which of the following best describes an example of political issues to consider when creating a forecast?

   a. The CEO of Smith Corona typewriters not considering the impact of computers in business.
   b. The federal breakup of Bell Telephone.
   c. The geographical differences between Dallas, TX and Boston, MA.
   d. Market demand for microwave ovens during the 1950s.
   e. Government subsidies offered for the development of new products.

5. Which is not one of the four basic forecasting methodologies defined by Chopra and Meindl at Northwestern University?

    a. Time series
    b. Extrapolators
    c. Qualitative
    d. Simulation
    e. Causal

6. In forecast optimization, all parties involved must be using the same _____, and understand each other's concerns, contributions, and expectations.

    a. Language
    b. Software
    c. Techniques
    d. Methods
    e. Databases

7. Which is not one of the five viewpoints of the future?

    a. Extrapolators
    b. Intuitors
    c. System designer
    d. Pattern analysts
    e. Goal analysts

8. Which is the additional factor that must be considered when forecasting on an international level versus an organizational level?

    a. Location
    b. Geography
    c. Technology
    d. Culture
    e. Logistics

9. Often, when different divisions within the same company use different methods, software and databases to forecast it creates?

    a. Environmental issues
    b. Isolated islands of information

c. Functionalist syndrome

d. Legal issues

e. A strong forecast

10. Which ERP software system was used in the HP case study?

a. SAP

b. Oracle

c. SAGE

d. Microsoft dynamics

e. Infor

11. What cost might go up in Walmart choosing to place orders every two weeks, rather than by month?

a. Holding costs

b. Fixed costs

c. Ordering costs

d. Safety stock costs

e. Total costs

12. Which is true for the top-down approach?

a. Large number of forecasters were involved.

b. Historical data is usually lost or incomplete.

c. Proper for specific promotional products and effective in planning for warehousing, manufacturing, and transportation.

d. Forecast on an aggregate level by using basic inputs such as historical data and promotion effects.

13. Which of the following is not true when creating a good forecast?

a. Aggregate data should be used for historic information.

b. Original forecasts should be retained and regularly measured for errors using various types of auditing techniques.

c. Focus on short-range forecasts.

d. Capture and use as much source data as possible.

e. Forecast product families wherever possible.

14. Which is not one of the main factors affecting forecast accuracy on an organizational level?

    a. Sales and marketing involvement
    b. Forecasting team structure
    c. Transportation involvement
    d. Data input
    e. Sales and operation planning

15. You have a forecasting viewpoint in line with counter-punchers. Which technique would you most likely use?

    a. Stakeholder analysis
    b. Nominal group analysis
    c. Precursor trend analysis
    d. Feedback models
    e. Cross-impact analysis

CHAPTER 4

Inventory Management

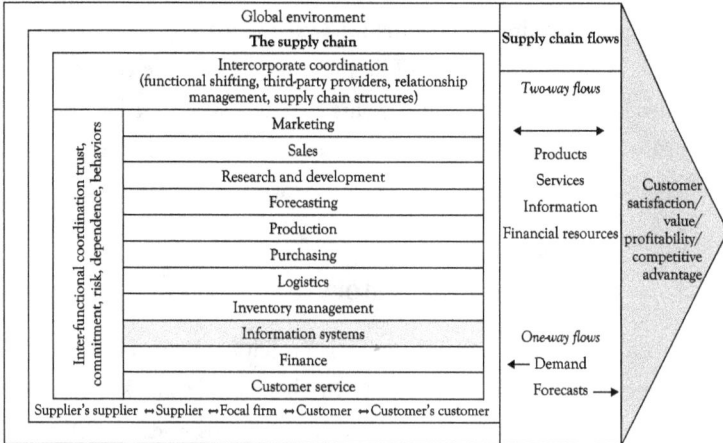

Chapter Objectives

- Define inventory management
- Explore the implications of inventory management to the supply chain
- Discuss the tools and techniques used in inventory management
- Explore factors that directly affect inventory management
- Focus on practice
- Applied inventory management review using mini-cases
- Examine trends in inventory management
- Learn from an economic order quantity example

It is very important for a company to successfully manage its inventory using all the techniques that it has available and those the firm sees fit for its type of business. By doing this, the company can lower costs such as overhead costs and increase customer satisfaction by improving inventory availability. Both *physical* and *logical* inventories require accurate and up-to-date information in order to be managed adequately. Carrying the right amount of inventory and ensuring that neither overstocking nor short-ages occur is the ultimate goal of inventory management. Strong inventory control is also dependent on accurate forecasts and timely replenishments.

Managed and organized information leads to better forecasting, improved inventory turns, lower costs, system efficiencies, increased customer satisfaction, and the list goes on. Information systems are established and maintained in a variety of ways. A company must ascertain its needs and develop or acquire an information system that supports its current and future business strategies. While these systems can be costly, a company must weigh the costs and benefits and determine the best solution to meet their goals. Nonetheless, a company must manage information to be efficient and ultimately to remain competitive in today's marketplace.

History

It has been said that war brings with it atrocities; however, sometimes great progress is achieved out of the mechanics of war. World War II was the principal creator of the science of operations research (OR). OR development began in the United Kingdom and later spilled over to the United States, where, in the early 1950s industrial operations grew. With this growth, inventory policies took a central stage within organizations due to inter- and intradepartmental complexities.

- The production department strove for efficiency, which demanded uninterrupted production runs, which meant a large inventory of work in process, as well as finished goods.
- Marketing wanted to provide customers with immediate delivery of goods, therefore demanded a large and diverse inventory.
- Finance wanted to minimize inventory balances in order to reduce capital blockage and to stabilize labor, which required goods to be produced for inventory at slack periods.

These issues gave rise to a major question: What inventory policy is best for the organization?

To address such questions, organizations needed a way to balance the overall business strategy of an organization as well as the objectives of individual departments. This need gave birth to the science of inventory management, a process to optimize the production and movement of raw materials, semifinished and finished products while meeting the financial and economic requirements of the firm.

Solutions to deal with problems of inventory management were developed as far back as 1915 by F. W. Harris. He developed the economic-lot-size equation. This equation sought to minimize the sum of inventory carrying cost and setup cost related to production and inventory control, when demands were certain. However, it was only in the early 1960s that concepts such as inventory forecasting and safety stock were introduced to help deal with fluctuating demands.

What Is Inventory Management?

Inventory management encompasses processes that ensure product availability while reducing investment costs. For most companies, there are two forms of inventory:

- **Physical inventory** includes all the materials that are tangible and required to fabricate the final product. And, the final product, including final pack-out materials.
- **Logical inventory** includes databases, inventory tracking software, and other such intangible assets.

Proper synchronization of these two inventories is essential for proper management of company assets. Inventory management also involves identifying the most effective source of supply for each item in each stocking location. Forecasting and replenishment are also integral to inventory management.

Why Do We Need Inventory Management?

Inventory is the **largest** and most difficult asset to manage for any organization. Improper management of inventory may lead to:

- **Overstocking**: Excess inventory can lead to increased costs, capital intensity, and potential obsolescence of stock, ultimately reducing the *flexibility* and *profitability* of the firm.

- **Shortages**: It is possible that some items are not available to be shipped in a timely manner to meet the customer's order requirements; this is considered an inventory shortage. In some cases, the inventory may be available but not traceable because of poor information control and/or availability. In either case, the organization risks disappointing the customer and potentially damaging its reputation, breaching contractual obligations or, worst case, permanently losing a customer.
- **Inaccurate information in logical inventory**: This inaccuracy can lead to inaccurate forecasting, as well as not being able to locate inventory that is actually available, overstocking or shortages of all types of inventory: raw materials, work-in-process, and finished goods.
- **Unsatisfactory Return on investment (ROI)**: The inventory holding costs may overshadow any profits earned.

How Does Inventory Management Help Us?

The following are benefits of proper management of inventory:

- **Better forecasting**: Accurate inventory information improves forecasting capabilities. This in turn can improve customer service and can reduce instances of overstocking and/or shortages.
- **Improved financial returns by reducing costs**: Inventory control activities are costly. Properly managed inventory reduces these costs. There are several different financial costs involved:
  - Cost of stocking and distributing materials;
  - Rent and utility expenses of warehouse;
  - Insurance and taxes on physical inventory;
  - Capital invested in inventory.
- **Identification of crucial products**: Better management can help differentiate between types of inventory items based on importance, customer category, and so on.
- **Ability to support JIT**: Properly managed inventory is essentially the same as having a JIT inventory process.

Factors Affecting Inventory Management

Despite the extensive coverage afforded to asset decisions in financial management literature and education, there tends to be one glaring shortcoming—inventory management The management of cash, physical capital assets, and, to a somewhat lesser extent, receivables is dealt with extensively. This omission cannot be defended by claiming that inventory is a relatively insignificant asset. On the contrary, even in this time-of-service industry domination, inventory management has important ramifications within any economy.

There are some major factors that have an impact on the management of inventory. Some of these overlooked factors are cost, quality, control, order size, and plant capacity.

Cost

Commodity prices can vary dramatically over a relatively short period of time. A strong expectation of rising prices could lead to an immediate, above-normal inventory buildup of the affected raw material. On the other hand, a strong expectation of falling prices might lead to an above-normal inventory stock reduction. A purchasing manager should compare the incremental carrying costs of larger inventory stocks to the expected price increase. The probability of error in all price expectations must, of course, also be kept in mind.

Order Size

There are various costs incurred each time an order is placed with a manufacturer, including delivery charges, handling costs, and paperwork expenses. It behooves a distributor to minimize the frequency of placing orders to hold down ordering costs. However, infrequent ordering necessitates large-order sizes, thereby leading to greater inventory stocks and an increase in carrying costs. Manufacturing firms also place orders for goods, particularly raw materials, and parts for use in production. By placing large orders, a manufacturer can, in essence, utilize inventory to minimize ordering costs. But again, inventory carrying costs must be incorporated into such a decision. It is the *trade-off* between ordering cost and carrying cost.

Forecasting

The forecasting function seeks to predict future demand. Forecasting is important in determining capacity, tooling, and personnel requirements.

Capacity Planning

Capacity planning is critical to production planning. Demands have to be anticipated: How far into the future should we go? The size of the capacity increment depends on the flexibility of the equipment we choose: Should we add capacity by expanding an existing facility, or should we build/buy/ lease a new one? It is often more expensive to build a new facility than to expand an existing one, but a new facility can often lead to other efficiencies. Again, there are many trade-offs that must be considered.

Production Scheduling

Production planning is another key element in the inventory management process. Continuous process manufacturers often produce a mix of products, one at a time, using the same equipment and facilities. Each time a different product is to be produced, it is necessary to stop the production process and make adjustments before proceeding. The costs of shutdown and adjustments, which are referred to as changeover costs, can be high. Production time is lost while the facilities are closed down, and labor costs must be expended to make the necessary adjustments. As a consequence of the changeover costs, businesses try to find ways to minimize the number of changeovers. One of the ways of achieving this goal is through the use of inventory management. Simply put, a company can choose to make many short production runs on each product in the mix, thereby incurring many changeovers and having smaller lots in inventory, or it can opt for long production runs and very few changeovers and increasing inventory lots. The economic order quantity (EOQ) model helps managers find the breakeven point for this situation.

Tools and Techniques of Inventory Management

There are many mathematical models for inventory control that can be used to determine the best strategy for inventory management.

Some of the oldest and simplest models include EOQ and Wagner–Whitin procedure. Today most of the industries are using techniques like manufacturing resource planning (MRP II), JIT and/or ERP, which is the next-generation MRP II.

The EOQ model is the order quantity at which the combination of ordering costs and inventory carrying costs is minimized. It is the most cost-effective quantity to purchase or produce for each replenishment. The EOQ model is applicable if demand for an item has a *constant rate* and the *entire quantity ordered arrives in inventory at one point in time*. EOQ calculations are frequently used in business by production, purchasing and inventory managers. This tool provides everything it takes to make reliable calculations. In addition, it automatically computes the reorder point (the inventory level at which new orders must be placed) and order cycle time, including consideration for any applicable lead times and/or safety stock requirements. See also the section on Supply Chain Trade-offs.

The Wagner–Whitin **procedure** assumes deterministic demand and deterministic production. It is better suited for purchasing than a production system.

MRP-II is used in many industries. It is a computational system that utilizes data management through an integrated information system. Planning and scheduling is based on historical data, forecasts, system constraints, and other such variables. Use of the MRP in conjunction with product bills of material (BOMs) can forecast materials requirements on a lot basis—known as material requirements planning.

ERP combines all departmental information together into a single, integrated information system so that the various departments can easily share information and communicate with each other. This integrated approach of centralized databases reduces duplicate and/or conflicting information caused when departments are responsible for "islands of information" that are not interconnected within the organization.

JIT inventory, as the title indicates, works on a real-time working environment basis. It assumes zero defects, small lot sizes, reduced set ups, and breakdowns, as well as minimal lead times. The goal of JIT is to reduce in-process inventory and the carrying costs associated with increased inventories.

In most manufacturing systems, a small fraction of purchased parts represents the largest portion of the firm's purchasing expenditures, which can also be referred to as the "Pareto" or "80/20" rule. In order to differentiate parts based on importance and requirements, many firms use an **ABC classification** system to identify purchased parts and materials. Items classified as "A" category parts make up generally 5 to 10 percent of the individual parts, yet collectively account for 75 to 80 percent of total annual expenditures. "B" category parts represent the next 10 to 15 percent and generally account for 10 to 15 percent of total annual expenditures. "C" category items represent the bottom 80 percent and account for only 10 percent of total annual expenditures.

These are some of the techniques used for inventory control management, however, in today's world ERP (which can include MRP) and JIT tend to be the most widely used.

Focus on Practice

As a matter of practice and implementation, there are many firms that have used MRP for years; however, because of upper management pressure, they are now moving to JIT. This brings up the issue of how to move employees and production systems from an MRP environment that has become ingrained in the corporate culture to something new. The simplest approach is to continue to use MRP, but move from large, fixed-order quantities to smaller quantities, the goal being a lot size of 1. Continue this process until you have moved all MRP lots to a lot-for-lot (LFL) strategy. After LFL has been used for a period of time, congratulate your employees on their embracing of JIT concepts (which is basically what they have been doing). At this point, it is much easier to transition to a true JIT environment, than an all-or-nothing or "cold turkey" approach.

Intensification in Inventory Management Use

Retailers continue looking for an optimal blend of art and science to conduct inventory management activities. They have spent time, money, and resources instituting fundamental techniques, establishing inventory control and aligning their assortments. The marketplace continues to become increasingly competitive and executing the basics compared with rivals may no longer be enough. For that reason, more inventory management techniques and practices are being used and the number is expected to grow. This growth is corroborated in a survey performed by Bearingpoint Inc. in 2003 on retail industries in the United States including department, big box, specialty, drug, and home improvement stores (www.bearingpoint.com). They found that 51 percent of the participants generate more than $500 million or more in annual sales and operate 100 stores or more.

In the survey, respondents showed that communications and shared information between retailers and their vendor partners had increased by 18 percent over 2002. This is shown in the following Figure 4.1.

The percentage of companies that shared inventory information was 76 percent. The three most used methods of sharing information and managing product inventory were *category management* (management of product categories as strategic business units), *automatic replenishment*, and *model stock level* with 67, 61, and 59 percent, respectively (see Figure 4.2).

Major obstacles faced by retailers in maintaining inventory integrity were rated by each organization on a scale from 1 to 10 (rating of 10 signifies "extremely dramatic impact"). The result was that the three major obstacles were identified: receiving, selling, and physical inventory counting errors, all with values of more than 6.4. This is detailed in Figure 4.3.

Almost all retailers agree that in order to reduce those errors they need to apply better employee training on policies and procedures, organization education, continue implementation in barcode scanning, and establish specialty measurements in terms of accuracy (see Figure 4.4).

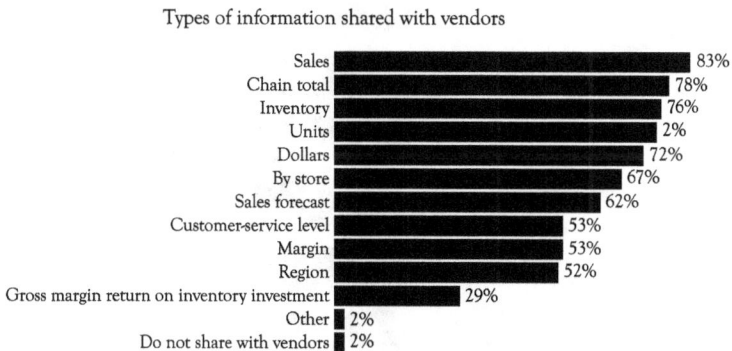

Types of information shared with vendors

Category	Percentage
Sales	83%
Chain total	78%
Inventory	76%
Units	2%
Dollars	72%
By store	67%
Sales forecast	62%
Customer-service level	53%
Margin	53%
Region	52%
Gross margin return on inventory investment	29%
Other	2%
Do not share with vendors	2%

Figure 4.1 Types of information shared with vendors

Methods of managing product inventory

Category management	67%
Automatic replenishment	61%
Model stock levels	59%
Vendor managed inventory	48%
Scale bases trading	40%
Collaborative planning and forecasting Replenishment	39%
Consignment	35%
Efficient consumer report	26%
Some other programs that was not mentioned	5%

Figure 4.2 Methods of managing product inventory

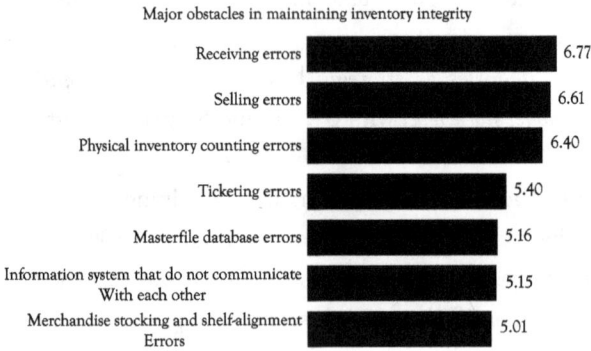

Major obstacles in maintaining inventory integrity

Receiving errors	6.77
Selling errors	6.61
Physical inventory counting errors	6.40
Ticketing errors	5.40
Masterfile database errors	5.16
Information system that do not communicate With each other	5.15
Merchandise stocking and shelf-alignment Errors	5.01

Figure 4.3 Obstacles in maintaining inventory integrity

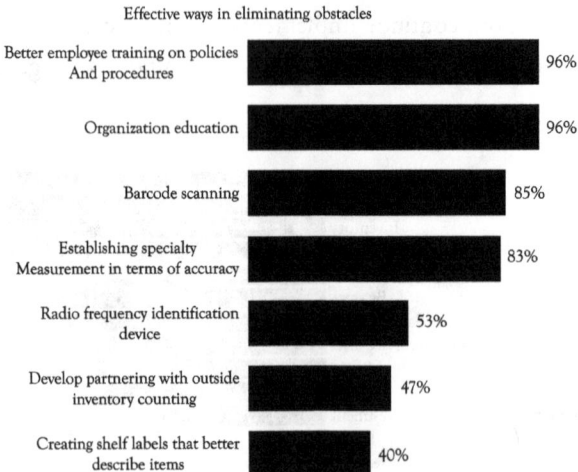

Effective ways in eliminating obstacles

Better employee training on policies And procedures	96%
Organization education	96%
Barcode scanning	85%
Establishing specialty Measurement in terms of accuracy	83%
Radio frequency identification device	53%
Develop partnering with outside inventory counting	47%
Creating shelf labels that better describe items	40%

Figure 4.4 Ways to eliminate obstacles

Mini-Case Examples of Implementation

Companies around the world have been successful implementing inventory management practices and techniques.

Walmart

Walmart's success is not just due to offering lower prices to the customer; it is also attributed to applying inventory management (only having in stock what people want). By electronically linking to their suppliers through EDI and their cross-docking strategy, Walmart and their suppliers gain advantages from "just-in-time" inventory control. The process is also streamlined through the elimination of paperwork from the stock reordering process, and the consequent elimination of processes associated with sorting, mailing, and storing of paper-based transactions. Walmart savings have been approximately $180 million by reducing its inventory and thus the annual cost of carrying excess inventory.

Home Depot

The Home Depot formula for success is a warehouse store format that features everyday low pricing, extraordinary customer service, quality products, and a large assortment of items. Price is a critical factor and sourcing; procurement and inventory management play important roles in the company's overall strategy. Home Depot moves over 85 percent of its merchandise directly from supplier to store, avoiding warehousing altogether. In addition, Home Depot developed a forecasting system internally that uses two years of point-of-sale (POS) data and provides replenishment planning, so that inventory threshold levels can be set, and vendor lead times accounted for. Home Depot's profit rose over 15 percent with all the improvements.

Littlewoods Stores in the United Kingdom

Littlewoods Stores operates more than 250 locations across the United Kingdom. The retail clothing industry is highly competitive and for that reason, Littlewoods began initiatives to improve their supply chain and specifically to deal with an overstocking problem. They implemented a data warehouse system, Decision Support System (DSS), and other software that transformed the business. The results included a 20 percent inventory reduction, 2 percent increase in margins, improvements in inventory turns, a 40 percent increase in staff productivity, and a 59 to 85 percent increase in cross-docking efficiency.

7-Eleven

7-Eleven is the United States' number one convenience-store chain in revenues. To compete more effectively, they rolled out an inventory management and sales data system that not only made the most of its limited shelf space and product assortment but also moved new products into stores and improved its position with its supplier. Using sales and inventory data, they handed over two dozen new products to store managers weekly including fresh and perishable food and were able to optimize sales and improve their inventory. 7-Eleven has grown to $10 billion in U.S. sales and $33 billion worldwide with all improvements.

Arizona Public Service (APS)

APS is the largest utility provider in Arizona, serving 705,000 customers and generating $1.7 billion in revenues annually. APS decided to scrutinize its supply chain for ways to increase efficiency and invest in new technology to support management of materials and services. They developed an electronic system that enables buyers and other company personnel to buy products and services through the streamlined processes of three online software modules (Material Catalog, Description Buy, and Express Buy). The time spent on improving the supply chain permitted APS to trim inventory by 25 percent and reduce purchasing cost by 5 percent. In turn, APS reduced the consumer electric rate by 5 percent.

Numerous other companies such as General Motors, Toyota (the leader in JIT), JCPenney, the U.S. Department of Defense, and so on are applying inventory management to improve customer service levels, warehouse efficiency, and overall profit. In general, American businesses have succeeded in applying various inventory management techniques. The U.S. Department of Commerce reported that from 1981 to 2000, inventory as a percentage of GDP fell 54.2 percent, from 8.3 to 3.8 percent.

The greatest challenge, by far, involves getting associates in different parts of the supply chain to work together. That's because many organizations still operate in a functional cost manner, where managers are rewarded for improving performance only within their own internal group.

Trends in Inventory Control

Companies are now seeing that collaboration between suppliers and vendors is important to making the supply chain successful. This idea of working together in a healthy relationship is driving what is being developed for the future of inventory management.

EDI is helping many businesses share data and improve inventory control. By utilizing EDI, a supplier can access their customers' inventory data and know when their inventory needs replenishing and can adjust their near-term manufacturing forecast plan using this information. When a company needs to place an order, they can do this through an EDI system and avoid a paper trail of purchase orders because the system will automatically save the information. It provides faster communication from one entity to another, and companies can access real-time data.

Vendor-managed inventory (VMI) is now being more readily used. Using a VMI program, a company outsources its inventory control to their supplier. VMI programs can result in inventory reduction, owing to the supplier handling inventory tracking and replenishment planning.

Scan-based trading (SBT) is mainly used by supermarkets; however, the concept is growing in popularity with retailers such as Do It Yourself (DIY) stores. This concept uses daily point of sale scan data to manage payment and replenishment of goods. The system allows for a perpetual inventory count; when an item is scanned at checkout, the program picks it up and adjusts the inventory accordingly. The difference in this system compared to other perpetual inventory control is that the supplier still owns the goods until the item is scanned; ownership of the goods passes at the time of the sale to the final consumer. At the time of sale, the title of the goods passes from the manufacturer, to the retailer, and, ultimately, to the consumer, all of which occur simultaneously. The retailer is obligated to pay for the goods, generally 7 to 10 days after the sale to the consumer. The supermarket acts like a warehouse for the manufacturer. The supplier gets real-time information on when their products are bought and can schedule their deliveries based on how much of an item remains in the store. SBT can reduce inventories, cut labor costs, streamline distribution, and maintain the optimal amount of inventory, saving money for both the supplier and the store. It should be noted, in this type of situation, that the burden of inventory carrying costs moves from the retailer to the manufacturer.

Collaborative planning, forecasting, and replenishment (CPFR) combines EDI and VMI. It is different because it allows more shared information between two entities and increases collaboration. It links the supply and demand of a product so that the retailer is more involved in the supply chain because both companies will be able to see the entire supply chain from one end to the other. The final retailer will be able to be involved from the manufacturing of raw materials to the final product. All the suppliers that are involved in the process of making an item are linked together and can get information about the other. This helps to determine shortcomings of material of any manufacturer in the chain so that companies can plan accordingly.

Owing to the heightened responsibility of both the supplier and vendor, both have had to accommodate each other. This relationship is becoming much more important and as such, the customer experience is being elevated. This is being done by having in-store KIOSKS or a detailed website where customers can get information and order products. Some companies have gone as far as to let the customer personalize their products to fit their needs. By doing this, the vendor is better able to track the interest of the product with what is actually being ordered.

A technology that has started to emerge to help with inventory management is **radio frequency identification** (RFID). RFID uses a computer chip and reader to let the user know when an item has arrived at an entrance and when it leaves an exit. Walmart first started to use this back in 2000 for individual items but dropped the study and decided it would be better to track pallets of goods. This has been the trend in industry as of this time. Until costs are reduced substantially, RFID at the pallet level is as detailed as tracking will get.

All the programs are used to keep real-time data on inventory. A company and its supplier will know when it is running short on inventory, which means that the cycle time in ordering is becoming shorter, more frequent with smaller lots. This type of situation helps both parties involved. It creates a continuous and steady flow of work for the supplier instead of having major peaks and lows and a retailer will know that its inventory is being taken care of.

Supply Chain Trade-Offs

Interactive relationships among the various members of the supply chain mean that a decision by one member can directly and severely impact another member. In this chapter, we have discussed EOQ. As a way of illustrating how to perform EOQ analysis and also how SCM decisions can impact various members of the supply chain, consider the following EOQ example.

The EOQ formula takes the total cost formula above and determines which quantity (Q) minimizes both the carrying and ordering costs. Graphically, this can be seen in Figures 4.5 and 4.6.

The way to find this optimal Q is to take the total cost curve, take the first derivative with respect to Q and set it equal to zero. Solving for

$$Q_{crr} = \sqrt{\frac{2DS}{H}} = \sqrt{\frac{2(\text{Annual Demand})(\text{Order Setup Cost})}{\text{Annual Holding Cost}}}$$

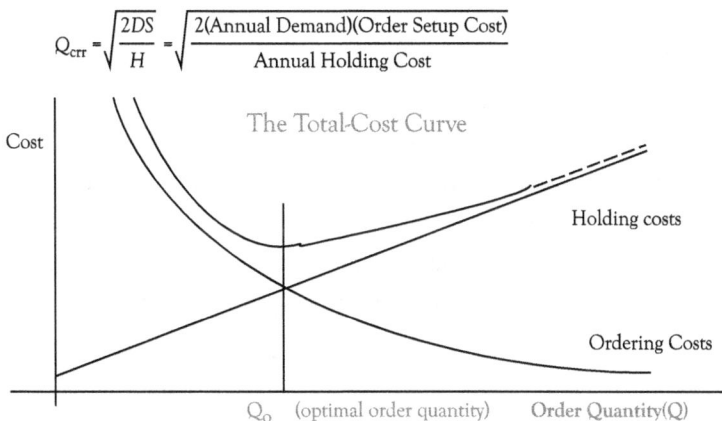

Figure 4.5 The basics of EOQ

$$\text{Total cost} = \begin{array}{c}\text{Annual}\\\text{carrying}\\\text{cost}\end{array} + \begin{array}{c}\text{Annual}\\\text{ordering}\\\text{cost}\end{array}$$

$$TC = \frac{Q}{2}H + \frac{D}{Q}S$$

Q–Lot size of the order
H–Average annual
　holding cost per unit
D–Annual demand
S–Cost per order

$Q/2$ = Average inventory
on hand

D/Q = Number of orders
per year

Figure 4.6 Necessary EOQ formulations

Q gives the Q_{opt} listed at the top of Figure 4.5. Given this information, we can now solve some problems and see what the implications are of various EOQ strategies.

EOQ Problem Set

A local retiree who is a woodworker has contracted to manufacture a small wooden souvenir item for sale at the hospitality booth at the local visitors' center. The manager of that booth is agreeable to the woodworker delivering finished goods at the shop owner's convenience. The items are relatively small and lightweight, so the primary cost of shipping is the relatively fixed cost of a trip across town. Relevant data for the shop are as follows:

- Annual demand (D) = 3,500 units
- Ordering (shipping) cost (S) = $12 per order (this ordering cost basically consists of loading the items into a 1956 GMC pickup truck and filling it up with gas for the roundtrip drive from the outskirts of town where the retiree lives).
- Holding cost (H) = $0.50 per unit per year (this cost is low because it consists of the retiree storing the souvenirs in the basement of his house).

At first, the manager of the hospitality booth doesn't care when the deliveries occur. Thus, the retiree decides to deliver the items in such a way as to reduce his total costs. Remembering his EOQ equations from his former job, he does the following:

- $Q_{opt} = \sqrt{\dfrac{2DS}{H}} = \sqrt{\dfrac{2 \times 3500 \times 12}{0.5}} = 410$

Thus, the retiree will wait until they have built 410 souvenirs, then load the truck and drive to the store. Now given this optimal Q, what are the retiree's total annual costs?

- The **ordering cost** is $\dfrac{DS}{Q} = \dfrac{3500 \times 12}{410} = \$102$

- The **holding cost** is $\dfrac{QH}{2} = \dfrac{410 \times 0.5}{2} = \$102.5$

- The **total cost** is $\dfrac{QH}{2} + \dfrac{DS}{Q} = 102 + 102.5 = \$204.50$

This continues for a while until the manager at the hospitality booth gets tired of receiving shipments at different times from all the vendors. The manager then asks all the vendors to make deliveries once a month. Before agreeing, the retiree checks the costs of this new requirement.

First, the retiree must determine what the new Q is. Since $D/Q = 12$ (once a month), and demand has not changed, the retiree determines that the new Q is 292 instead of 410. Given that the following is true,

- The **ordering cost** is $\dfrac{DS}{Q} = \dfrac{3500 \times 12}{292} = \$144$

- The **holding cost** is $\dfrac{QH}{2} = \dfrac{292 \times 0.5}{2} = \$72.92$

- The **total cost** is $\dfrac{QH}{2} + \dfrac{DS}{Q} = 144 + 72.92 = \$216.92$

The difference between this cost and the first optimal cost is $216.92 - 204.50 = 12.42$, so the retiree decides to agree to the manager's request.

The manager of the hospitality booth has been taking MBA courses at Wright State University and learns about the wonders of JIT. The manager realizes that if all his suppliers made deliveries once a week then he wouldn't need the back room to store inventory. Instead, he could knock out the wall and nearly double his sales floor, possibly increasing sales. Or, he could not use the back room at all and sell it to someone else to reduce costs. Either way he comes out ahead. Thus, he tells all the suppliers to make deliveries once a week.

The retiree goes back and assesses the costs of once-a-week delivery. First, the retiree must determine what the new Q is. Since $D/Q = 52$ (once a week), and demand has not changed, the retiree determines that the new Q is now 67. Given that, the following is true:

- The **ordering cost** is $\dfrac{DS}{Q} = \dfrac{3500 \times 12}{67} = \$624$

- The **holding cost** is $\dfrac{QH}{2} = \dfrac{67 \times 0.5}{2} = \$16.83$

- The **total cost** is $\dfrac{QH}{2} + \dfrac{DS}{Q} = 624 + 16.83 = \$640.83$

The difference between these costs and the first (optimal) costs is $640.83 - \$202.50 = \$436.33$. The retiree realizes that once-a-week delivery would each up all the profit he is making. Since he is only doing this for fun, the retiree decides not to supply the hospitality booth any more but to devote his leisure time to fishing.

This particular EOQ example illustrates the issues involved with JIT. The entire concept of JIT has been heralded for years as a way for firms to reduce inventory and thus reduce costs. This allows firm to increase ROI and other financial measures. As a general rule, larger firms have embraced JIT concepts and asked their suppliers (usually smaller firms) to provide them with JIT deliveries. While large firms view JIT positively as a means to reduce costs, as a general rule, smaller firms have a different view of JIT. They refer to it as "I get to hold your inventory" and the accompanying costs. Thus, supply chain managers need to understand that when implementing any new system (forecasting, planning and control, or distribution) they need to be aware of what the impact of that system will be to both upstream and downstream supply chain players. By incorporating those players in the initial planning and assessment, alternatives may be found. Even if no alternatives are found, at least the other members of the supply chain will know what is coming in plenty of time to adapt to the requisite changes.

Key Takeaways

- Strong inventory management protects the company from overstocking, shortages, inaccurate logical information, and unsatisfactory ROI.
- The results of good inventory management include, but are not limited to, better forecasting, improved financial returns by reducing costs, identification of crucial products, and the ability to support JIT strategies.
- The tools of inventory management include EOQ modeling, Wagner–Whiten procedure, MRP II, ERP, JIT, and ABC classification. If you are not familiar with any of these, it would be beneficial to learn about those and run analyses to determine if they would be beneficial to your organization.
- Trends in inventory control include EDI, VMI, SBT, CPFR, and RFID. By keeping up to date on what is happening with these trends through trade organizations, customer contacts, and so on, will give your company a competitive advantage. Even if you are not currently participating in these activities, you should be prepared in case you are asked to participate with any of your trading partners.

Reflection Points

1. What are the main types of inventory control methods used in your company? How are they managed? What areas of inventory control have been the same for a long time? Numerous changes in best practices in the recent past suggest that any processes that have not been evaluated and/or updated in the last 1 to 3 years are outdated.
2. Why has your firm adopted these inventory control methods? Was there an analysis of best methods or is it a case of "we've always done it this way?"
3. Has your company ever attempted to change inventory control methods? If so, how successful or unsuccessful was it? What were the key factors that led to that success or failure?

4. Do you or your team know how much your inventory control processes cost? All processes should undergo a cost/benefit analysis on a regular basis.

5. Are you outsourcing any portion of your inventory control processes or requirements? Why or why not?

6. Are your customers pushing inventory control responsibilities upstream in the supply chain, in other words, pushing the responsibilities and carrying costs back to you? Do you know how this is affecting your company operationally and financially? Understanding these effects will allow you to negotiate from a stronger position when propositions like these are made by your customers in the future.

Additional Resources

Bonabeu, E. 2002. "Predicting the Unpredictable." *Harvard Business Review 80,* no. 3, pp. 5–11.

Chopra, S. and P. Meindl. 2004. *Supply Chain Management: Strategy, Planning and Operatio*n, 2nd ed. New Jersey, NJ: Pearson.

Donnan, S. and P. Hines. 1999. "Designing a Supply Chain Change Process: A Food Distribution Case." *International Journal of Retail and Distribution Management.*

Hammond, J.H. and W.R. Obermayer. 1994. "Making Supply Meet Demand in an Uncertain World." *Harvard Business Review* 72, no. 3, pp. 83–93.

Handfield, R. 2003. *The* Profit-Leverage *Effect in Supply Chains.*

Jain, C.L. Fall 2003. "Business Forecasting in the 21st Century." *The Journal of Business Forecasting,* pp. 3–6.

Kolbasuk, M. May 22, 2000. "GM to Link Supply Chain With Inventory Management." Internet *Week,* no. 814, p. 13, 1/3 p, 1 c.

Mangan, J. and Lalwani, C. 2016. *Global Logistics and Supply Chain Management,* 3rd ed., p. 181. John Wiley & Sons.

North Carolina State University. n.d. *Supply Chain Resource Cooperative.* http:// scrc.ncsu.edu/public/DIRECTOR/dir031103.html.

Ritzman, L. and L. Krajewski. 2003. *Foundations of Operations Management.* New Jersey, NJ: Prentice Hall.

Schreibfeder, J. n.d. *The Mysterious Cost of Carrying Inventory.* https:// effectiveinventory.com/the-mysterious-cost-of-carrying-inventory/.

Schreibfeder, J. n.d. *What Is Effective Inventory Management?* https:// effectiveinventory.com/implementing-effective-inventory-management/.

Simchi-Levi, D. and P. Kaminsky. 2003. *Designing and Managing the Supply Chain Concepts, Strategies and Case Studies,* 2nd ed. Irwin: McGraw-Hill.

Toomey, J. 2000. *Inventory Management principles concepts and Techniques.* Boston: Kluwer Academic Publisher.

Viale, J. 1996. *Inventory Management.* California: Crips Publications, Inc.

Williams, D. 2004. *The Strategic Implications of* Wal-Mart's *RFID Mandate.* https://www.directionsmag.com/article/3471.

Worthen, B. January 15, 2003. "Hot Potato!" *CIO Magazine.*

Multiple Choice Questions

1. What is not one of the reasons we need inventory management?

    a. Overstocking

    b. Shortages

    c. Accurate information in logical inventory

    d. Unsatisfactory ROI

    e. Reductions in working capital

2. What was the principal creator of the science of operations research (OR)?

    a. Too many stockouts

    b. WWII

    c. SAP

    d. Arizona Public Service (APS)

    e. CPFR

3. Under which inventory management factor is there a *trade-off* between ordering cost and carrying cost?

    a. Forecasting

    b. Cost

    c. Capacity planning

    d. Production scheduling

    e. Order size

4. What is not one of the benefits of proper inventory management?

    a. Better forecasting

    b. Decreased ROI

    c. Improved financial returns by reducing costs

    d. Identification of crucial products

    e. Ability to support JIT

5. Under which inventory management factor is there a *trade-off* between lot size and changeover costs?

    a. Forecasting

    b. Cost

    c. Capacity planning

    d. Production scheduling

    e. Order size

6. What is the ultimate goal of inventory management?

    a. Carrying the right amount of inventory and ensuring that neither overstocking nor shortages occur.

    b. Having an order quantity at which the combination of ordering costs and inventory carrying costs is minimized.

    c. The incorporation of a computer chip and reader to let the user know when an item has arrived at an entrance and when it leaves an exit.

    d. Linking the supply and demand of a product so that the retailer is more involved in the supply chain because both companies will be able to see the entire supply chain from one end to the other.

    e. To make sure that forecasts are perfect in meeting demand.

7. Collaborative planning, forecasting, and replenishment (CPFR) combines _____ and _____ to allow more shared information between two entities and increases collaboration.

    a. Radio frequency identification; Vendor-managed inventory

    b. Scan-based trading; Vendor-managed inventory

    c. Electronic data interchange; Scan-based trading

    d. Vendor-managed inventory; Electronic data interchange

    e. Electronic data interchange; Radiofrequency identification

8. Which best describes when a company outsources its inventory control to their supplier?

    a. VMI

    b. EDI

    c. RFID

    d. CPFR

    e. SBT

9. Which is not an inventory management tool mentioned in the text?

    a. ABC classification

    b. EOQ modeling

    c. Cycle counts

    d. ERP

    e. MRP II

10. What was the main type of information shared between retailers and their vendor partners?

    a. Inventory

    b. Sales

    c. Dollars

    d. Units

    e. Chain total

11. Which best describes items that are not available to be shipped in a timely manner to meet the customer's order requirements?

    a. Overstocking

    b. Inaccurate information in logical inventory

    c. Reductions in working capital

    d. Shortages

    e. Unsatisfactory ROI

12. Walmart first started to use this back in 2000 for individual items but dropped the study and decided it would be better to track pallets of goods.

    a. ERP

    b. EOQ

    c. Cycle counts

    d. RFID

    e. ROI

13. What is not an example of financial costs that can be reduced to improve financial returns that was mentioned in the text?

   a. Cost of sales
   b. Rent and utility expenses of warehouse
   c. Cost of stocking and distributing materials
   d. Insurance and taxes on physical inventory
   e. Capital invested in inventory

14. What best describes when the inventory holding costs may overshadow any profits earned?

   a. Inaccurate information in logical inventory
   b. Unsatisfactory ROI
   c. Reductions in working capital
   d. Capacity planning
   e. Identification of crucial products

15. The EOQ formula takes the total cost formula and determines which quantity (Q) minimizes both _____ and _____.

   a. Value, risk
   b. Total cost, fixed cost
   c. Fixed cost, ordering cost
   d. Total cost, carrying cost
   e. Carrying cost, ordering cost

CHAPTER 5

Distribution

Physical distribution has three primary concerns.

- *Receiving* parts or finished goods
- *Storing* them until they are required
- *Delivering* them to the customer

The transfer of material from facility to facility, and ultimately to the customer, is the responsibility of the firm's distribution channel. A bottleneck in this process could have detrimental consequences, such as increasing lead time for completion of a product, which raises costs and reduces margins, and could potentially lose the sale and future patronage. Therefore, the company must not take this activity too lightly and should plan accordingly.

Supply chain managers must address several important distribution decisions. This includes which transport mode to use, the physical architecture of your distribution system (including the number and location of distribution warehouses) and whether to own or contract-out warehousing and transport.

Transportation

There are many different types of transportation available to businesses. The most common are seen in the following Figure 5.1. The figure also shows multimodal configurations. When two types or modes are combined, you have multimodal transport methods. For example, stocking trucks on a railcar for long-distance shipping is called piggybacking.

Birdy backing is the method of transportation that requires the transfer of containers from truck to plane (Birdyback n.d.). Fishy backing has to do with the transportation requirements involving the transfer of

Rail		Air
	Truck	
Water		Pipeline

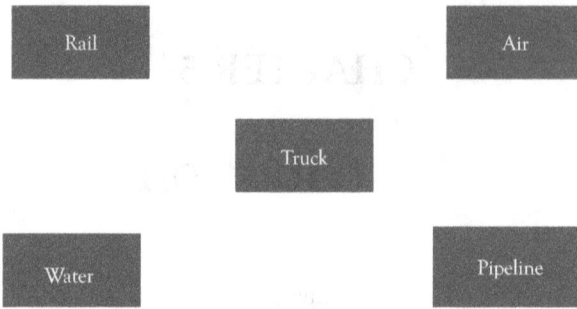

Figure 5.1 Transportation methods

containers from truck to ship (Fishyback n.d.). Other methods do exist, but their application is minuscule in scope when compared to the afore-mentioned. For example, in large urban areas, bike couriers are sometimes practical, due to the congestion of roads and proximity of customers. Even pipelines, which companies use for transportation of crude oil and natural gas from source to refineries, are limited in their availability. Thus, air, truck, rail, and water are the key transport methods used in most businesses.

> *Trucks* have the advantage of being flexible. They also provide low loss and damage transport along with tracking, accuracy, and a wide geographical coverage. Another advantage is that there is currently heavy price competition in the trucking industry; thus, driving down costs. Unfortunately, weather and traffic conditions delay truck shipments.

> *Railroads'* advantages are that they provide inexpensive transport for carload size lots. However, goods require more packing material and must allow for rough handling. While rail transport can be some-what slow, the cost savings can be fairly substantial. Firms should also look to freight forwarders, piggybacking trucks and double stacking containers for more opportunities for cost savings.

> *Water transport* is ideal for goods that are heavy, low value, and nonper-ishable. Of course, weather can be a problem and add to transport times. However, containerization (the process of combining several unitized loads into a single well-protected load) and improved ports allow for expansion in new products and markets.

Air transport is the transport method with the highest costs. Thus, it is only suitable for high value, urgent or perishable items. Of course, weight and locations are limited. However, it saves on inventory holding costs because of the reduced transport times. This method is becoming more important in international trade.

Pipeline is the transportation method chosen for solids, liquids, and gases that can be moved with pressure over long distances. This method is commonly used for the transport of oil and natural gas products.

In Europe, where the geography is more condensed and regulations permit high-speed rail systems, rail is preferable to truck on both time and cost. In developing countries, the road infrastructure may be so poor that rail is again preferable to trucks. Knowledge of the infrastructure in the area of operations is important to determining the best transportation methodology.

In addition, outsourcing should be considered for particular aspects in the distribution channel. While a company may have the equipment to transport materials from a manufacturing plant to the distribution center, it may not have the logistical capability to then deliver to its many customers. If it is international, then there might be a possibility that they lack the resources to effectively handle transportation in that country.

Delivery Methods

Once transportation decisions have been made, then delivery schedules must be set up. For most transportation modes there are two basic types of deliveries: direct and milk run.

Direct Deliveries

As the name implies, direct deliveries move goods from one origin facility to one receiving facility. Routing in this case is straightforward and usually consists of choosing the shortest direct path. Because of the direct nature of the transport, intermediary steps such as warehousing, shipment combination, and so on are removed.

Milk Runs

In bygone days, the milkman would deliver from a dairy store to multiple individual family homes. Hence, a milk run is one which delivers from a central origin to multiple locations. Milk runs are more complex than direct shipments. For example, decisions about quantities have to be made up front. Once this is determined, decisions must be made concerning the frequency of deliveries. Finally, scheduling must be done.

Delivery Sources

Customer deliveries can be made from either single-product locations or from distribution centers. Single-product locations are ideal if you are dealing with high volumes of product with predictable demand. In that case, the production facility or warehouse can deliver to customers in large bulk quantities thus allowing for large economies of scale.

However, distribution centers (DCs) tend to be the primary facilities for most physical distribution structures because bulk quantities of different products must be combined in multiple ways and quantities to serve a large number of customers, which may be located a great distance from the suppliers. DCs can warehouse inventory for future shipment, or they can be used for crossdocking. This is a technique that was pioneered by Walmart and has been embraced by many other firms. Because of its widespread use, we will assess it in more detail.

Crossdocking

When it comes to distribution techniques, crossdocking can be a strategic weapon in a successful physical distribution design, which is heavily dependent upon execution and integration. Crossdocking can be viewed in several different ways. One might view it as combining both warehouse and distribution center functions. Another way of viewing it is as warehousing without inventory.

Crossdocks are essentially transshipment facilities to which trucks arrive with goods that must be sorted, consolidated with other products, and loaded onto outbound trucks as shown in Figure 5.2. Outbound

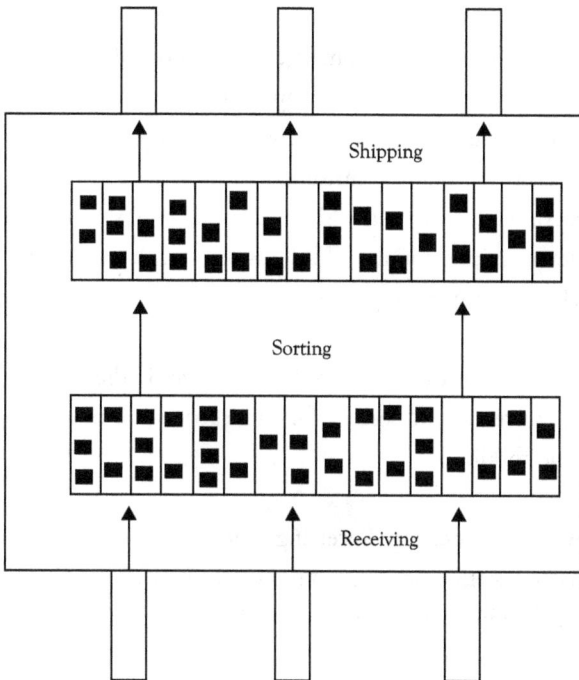

Figure 5.2 Crossdocking

trucks may be headed for a manufacturing site, a retail outlet, or another crossdock, depending on the specific application.

Types of Crossdocking

The term "crossdocking" has been used to describe several different types of operations, all of which involve the rapid consolidation and shipment of products:

- **Manufacturing crossdocking**: Receiving and consolidating inbound supplies to support JIT manufacturing. For example, a manufacturer might lease a warehouse close to its plant in order to prepare subassemblies or consolidate kits of parts. Because demand for the parts is known, say from the output of an MRP system, there is no need to maintain stock.
- **Distributor crossdocking**: Consolidating inbound products from different vendors into a multi-SKU (Stock Keeping

Unit) pallet, which is delivered as soon as the last product is received. For example, computer distributors often source components from different manufacturers and consolidate them into one shipment in merge-in-transit centers, before delivering them to the customer.

- **Transportation crossdocking**: Consolidating shipments from different shippers in the LTL (Less than truckload) and small package industries to gain economies of scale.

For small package carriers, material movement in the crossdock is by a network of conveyors and sorters; for LTL carriers it is mostly by manual handling and forklifts.

- **Retail crossdocking**: Receiving product from multiple vendors and sorting onto outbound trucks for different stores. Crossdocking has been cited as a major reason Walmart surpassed Kmart in retail sales in the 1980s.
- **Opportunistic crossdocking**: In any warehouse, transferring an item directly from the receiving dock to the shipping dock to meet a known demand.

Ways to successfully implement crossdocking:

- Vendor cooperation
- Integrated information system with vendors
- High visibility and control
- Strong quality control program for the inbound
- Partnership with the vendors

Advantages of crossdocking:

- Reduced handling costs
- Reduced inventory carrying costs
- Reduced cycle time/improved transit time
- Improved flexibility in opting for transportation mode
- Improved customer service
- Reduced space utilization

Architecture

Depending on the goals of the organization, there are many different types of ways that the supply chain's distribution system may be structured. If the firm is attempting to provide a high level of customer service with quick delivery times, then they may opt to have a decentralized hierarchy with many distribution centers scattered across the country. While this may incur additional costs, such as increased inventory and overhead from the additional facilities, it will almost ensure that they will be able to achieve their goals. If cost is the main driver, then a centralized warehouse and distribution network may be preferred, as this type of structure will allow for cost savings at the expense of delivery times.

Also, given the nature of the company's industry and products, the distribution system must be accommodating to factors of production. For industries that produce products with bulky raw materials that undergo a weight-losing process (e.g., drilling, cutting, and stamping of raw iron into parts), manufacturing plants and distribution centers must be relatively close to the source of these inputs. Conversely, products that are subject to weight-gaining activities (e.g., final assembly), where it is more economical to move the components than the final product, must be located toward the end of the supply chain near the consumer. Examples of these two concepts can be better explained by the steel industry and aerospace, where due to the bulk of iron ore, steel plants are located near the strip mines, and due to the size of jet fighters once finished, they are usually located near military facilities. A more extreme example of the latter would be the NASA program, where the space shuttle manufacturing facility is located approximately three miles away from the launch pad.

To summarize, when structuring your logistics and supply chain network, every structure is a variant of the extremes of centralized and decentralized. Both extremes have advantages. The key is to focus on the needs of your particular firm and its strategic position. Your distribution system's structure should follow from that.

Advantages of centralization include:

- Risk pooling/Variance reduction effect
- Economies of scale
- Economies of scope

- Learning/Experience curve
- Coordination advantages

Advantages of decentralization include:

- Product/Process improvements
  - Proximity to suppliers
- Customer satisfaction
  - Proximity to markets/customers
- Cost savings
  - Sourcing, Production, Logistics—Financing
- Risk diversification/Portfolio effect
  - Technology risk—Financial risk

Organizational Change

Steps for successfully altering an international supply chain's distribution system include:

- Conducting a comprehensive analysis of the infrastructure costs and customer service levels by channel, inventory levels, and product flow.
- Developing a strategy to meet customer expectations, product availability, and delivery timing with lower operating costs.
- Listing out the assumptions to be made at the planning stage.
- Adopting a risk management approach early in the process.
- Developing the target infrastructure to create a simpler and cost-effective supply chain that was scalable.
- Expecting the unexpected.
- Having the right personnel at the right place.
- Planning for change by balancing skills to unlock the complex combination of people and skills.
- Developing a thorough organizational structure by balancing internal and external resources via:
  - Steering group
  - Program management group

    o Business change group
    o Project management group
    o Project working group

As simple as many of these principles are, many will recognize just how often the basics are ignored, thus burning through a large investment with no hope of a realistic return. The too difficult or politically unacceptable projects might hold the secret to unlocking value. However, before embarking on any major distribution restructuring, a supply chain manager should determine the following:

The company must have adequate resources

- At senior management level;
- And at all subsequent levels according to where you are in the overall process.

Whatever the change in any business,

- People are at the center of it;
- Things will go wrong that are not planned for;
- Things usually get worse before they get better;
- You must maintain a sense of perspective through careful planning.

Clear metrics of success and benefits, as well as a method of tracking those successes must be established and visible to all. The role of risk management (safety net) is never to be underestimated. Once these things are taken into consideration, the transition into a new system can take place more easily and effectively.

Outsourcing in Distribution

As previously discussed, outsourcing is being used a great deal in SCM. One of the major areas of SCM outsourcing is distribution, specifically logistics.

Third-Party Logistics (3PL)

There are many benefits to using 3PL to handle many logistical functions that go beyond cost, such as more flexibility and increased customer satisfaction. It allows for the company to not have to maintain a vast logistical network and tie up working capital. For example, Dell Computers has no internal delivery service to their customers, but by outsourcing to UPS, they are able to deliver machines to their customers overnight at a lower cost than they could ever provide.

Fourth-Party Logistics (4PL)

A 4PL offers expanded services in comparison to 3PLs, which only deal with one aspect of the clients business (logistics), while 4PLs often deal with inventory and vendor management. The result is a better solution for the client, with more reliable service and results. As a practical matter, most 3PLs have morphed into 4PLs.

Freight Forwarding

When dealing with international shipments, there are several extra facets to transportation, such as customs. This complicates the process and adds additional paperwork. As a result, many companies have outsourced international shipments to freight forwarders. Companies that already have an expansive logistics capability, such as FedEx and DHL, offer freight forwarding in these counties, often with little existing infrastructure. This allows for companies to not have to spend an exorbitant amount of money to develop their logistical capabilities in that country and provide a high level of customer service as well.

International Distribution and SCM

There are many benefits to moving operations offshore. Free trade zones are attractive locations for companies to develop manufacturing facilities, whereas they are able to avoid duties and tariffs on the inputs of production that are not resold into the host county. Companies are able to exploit the lower labor costs and other incentives, and still are able to produce the product and ship it anywhere they so desire.

Another reason for international expansion is the proximity to emerging markets. Developing countries often provide a lucrative opportunity to these firms, which are willing to forgo initial profits to reap greater returns further down the line. In these cases, the firms employ a market share strategy and wager that once the country becomes rather affluent, they will have a sizable foothold in the country and recover their initial costs.

Expansion into foreign countries, however, often brings about new issues regarding the supply chain. Several of the constants that are taken for granted in the United States are not present in many other nations.

- Within the United States, the logistics capabilities are second to none. The existence of a vast highway system allows for freedom of movement to all parts of the country. These also extend into neighboring countries to an extent, allowing for easy transportation by a single mode.
- In addition, there is an expansive rail network that allows for economical transportation of large quantities of goods to the major cities.
- Seaports have been built in all the major coastal cities, allowing for massive import/export operations and international trade.
- Airports are scattered across the nation, allowing overnight delivery to any part of the country. Some air service providers even offer deliveries within hours from one side of the country to the other, and to the major cities in-between.
- Also, there is an elaborate telecommunication network that allows for the flow of information. Cellular, broadband, Wi-Fi, and satellite communications allow for companies to exchange and track information regarding their products.
- Computers are networked together, so that people in different departments and even different cities can easily access information about a particular product.

Internationally, few nations have the capability discussed previously, and as a result, companies must adapt to the differences in their host country. Many countries lack the infrastructure, making transportation difficult. Such is the case in China, where two-thirds of the roads are unusable for modern trucks. As a result, its chemical industry is suffering, despite efforts of chemical manufacturers in China and the World Trade Organization. Utilities in many countries are not as sophisticated as those in the United States, and manufacturers may have to contend with rolling blackouts or brownouts. Infrastructure may not be as developed as well, and firms must account for that variability in their transit times. For example, many countries do not have cellular service, and lack the advanced communications for computers. Some countries, such as Russia after the revolution, even had problems with basic telephone service.

In addition, the culture and political landscape may not be very hospitable in those countries as initially thought. In Japan, bribery is considered a part of business, and a necessity in order to remain competitive. This is in stark contrast to business practices in the United States, a plight that the U.S. Olympic committee became all too familiar with after its bid for the winter games in Salt Lake City. Many Muslim countries have laws discriminating against women, so the company would be wise to take that into consideration before sending female expatriates oversees. Also, there might be some political instability that would affect the supply chain. Imagine a company losing a billion-dollar facility to foreign nationals, such as the case of Chevron Texaco, who temporarily lost control of its refinery operations in Nigeria after unarmed village women stormed pipeline stations. Such an action would have a severely detrimental effect on the entire network, and the company itself.

Thus, from a practical perspective SCM managers must accept that different aspects of managing inventory and distribution change when the distribution network moves from a domestic to a global structure. To summarize, higher inventories are a given because of the longer lead times and increased uncertainty. The lead times are longer because distances are longer, transportation is more costly and multiple modes are often required. As borders are crossed, delays are encountered as new documentation is needed.

Multiple borders and countries also bring up the issues of managing physical distribution facilities and employees with different cultures, laws, and languages. A simple issue such as taking an order can be complex when the order-processing center is in a different country than the ordering and the languages involved are different. All these issues combine, and service tends to be slower and more costly as buffer inventories are increased to keep service levels high.

Focus on Practice: European Methods of Integration

Europe has felt the effects of complex and overly complicated supply chain systems that have in the past required distribution centers in every country. These large, intricate systems have presented several problems for companies as they strive to stay competitive in the global marketplace. Several drivers are leading European companies toward integration of their physical distribution systems:

- Profit levels failing to meet management objectives.
- Operational performance varying widely by brand, business, or unit.
- Customer service levels not contributing to competitive differentiation.
- Inventory levels high and rising higher with a poor demand–supply balance.
- Suppliers and consumers not well linked to the overall company operations.
- Companies in industries with rapid growth in the late 1990s.
- Companies in traditionally low-growth sectors.
- Companies with multiple brands running separate operations.
- Multiple subsidiaries of multinational corporations.

Key Takeaways

- Physical distribution has three primary concerns: receiving, storing, and delivering.
- Methods of transportation include, but are not limited to, rail, water, truck, air, and pipeline. Infrastructure in each country you plan to do business within is extremely important. You should know the transportation capabilities of countries in which you plan to distribute or manufacture.

- Crossdocking can be a key ingredient to satisfying your customers. Manufacturing, distributor, transportation, retail, and opportunistic crossdocking are different methods that you can use to satisfy your customers' or your own needs or requirements.
- Outsourcing distribution is a strategic option that should be undertaken only after engaging in a detailed analysis of how your company will benefit and what the costs will be to your organization and even your customers. Outsourcing in this arena can significantly benefit your business strategies if administered correctly. Be certain to put processes in place to ensure the transparency of the 3PL or 4PL's activities and costs incurred on your behalf.

Reflection Points

1. What is the primary method of transportation that your firm uses in distribution? Why? How does this support your firm's competitive priorities?
2. Does your firm control its own distribution system, or does it outsource it? Why or why not?
3. Is your distribution network centralized or decentralized? How do you think your network's structure relates to the answers you gave in questions 1 and 2?
4. Does your firm utilize crossdocking? Have you been pleased with the results? Have those results been measured?

Additional Resources

Bartholdi, J.J., K.R. Gue, and K. Kang. 2001. "Throughput Models for Unit-Load Crossdocking." In *Review*.

Begley, T.M. and D.P. Boyd. Winter 2002. "The Need for a Corporate Global Mind-Set." *MIT Sloan Management Review*.

Birdyback. n.d. Monash Business School. www.monashedu/business/marketing/marketing-dictionary/b/birdyback (accessed April 8, 2021).

Bovet, D. January/February 2004. "Europe's New Growth Driver." *Supply Chain Management Review*.

Chopra, S. and P. Meindl. 2004. *Supply Chain Management: Strategy, Planning and Operation,* 2nd ed. Upper Saddle River, NJ: Pearson.

Donnan, S. and H. Peter. 1999. "Designing a Supply Chain Change Process: A Food Distribution Case." *International Journal of Retail & Distribution Management* 27, no. 10, pp. 409–420.

Duris, R. September 2003. "The Seven Deadly Sins of Supply Chain Management." Frontline Solutions.

Eisenhardt, K.M. Winter 2002. "Has Strategy Changed." *MIT Sloan Management Review.*

Fishyback. n.d. Monash Business School. www.monashedu/business/marketing/marketing-dictionary/f/fishyback (accessed April 8, 2021).

MacMillan, I.C., A.B. Van Putten, and R.G. McGrath. May 2003. "Global Gamesmanship." *Harvard Business Review.*

Napolitano, M. 2001. "Making the Move to Cross Docking." Warehousing Education and Research Council.

Olivia, R. and W. Noel. March/April 2009. "Managing Functional Biases in Organizational Forecasts: A Case Study of Consensus Forecasting in Supply Chain Planning." *Production and Operations Management 18, no. 2,* pp. 138–151.

Richardson, H.L. April 2004. "Execution at the Dock." *Logistics Today.*

Ritzman, L. and K. Lee. 2003. *Foundations of Operations Management.* Upper Saddle River, NJ: Pearson.

Schaer, B. 1997. "Implementing a Crossdocking Operation." *IIE Solutions,* no. 36, p. 34.

Simchi-Levi, D. and K. Philip. 2003. *Designing and Managing the Supply Chain Concepts, Strategies and Case Studies,* 2nd ed. Boston, MA: Irwin/McGraw-Hill.

Stalk, G., P. Evans, and L.E. Shulman. 1992. "Competing on Capabilities: The New Rules of Corporate Strategy." *Harvard Business Review,* no. 69, p. 57.

Toomey, J. 2000. *Inventory Management Principles Concepts and Techniques.* Boston, MA: Kluwer Academic Publisher.

Worthen, B. January 15, 2003. "Hot potato!" *CIO Magazine.*

Zwolinski, K. February 2003. "Changing Supplies." *Manufacturing Engineer.*

Multiple Choice Questions

1. Which of the following is not one of the main primary concerns of physical distribution?

   a. Pipeline
   b. Receiving

    c. Storing

    d. Delivering

2. This form of transportation includes the transfer of containers from truck to plane.

    a. Fishyback

    b. Piggyback

    c. Birdyback

    d. Air transport

    e. Rail

3. What is the most flexible form of transportation?

    a. Rail

    b. Truck

    c. Pipeline

    d. Air

    e. Water

4. Which transportation method is most suitable in Europe?

    a. Water

    b. Pipeline

    c. Truck

    d. Rail

    e. Air

5. What is a "milk run?"

    a. Movement of goods from one origin facility to one receiving facility.

    b. Combining both warehouse and distribution center functions.

    c. The delivery from a central origin to multiple locations.

    d. Receiving product from multiple vendors and sorting onto outbound trucks for different stores.

    e. In any warehouse, transferring an item directly from the receiving dock to the shipping dock to meet a known demand.

6. Which of the following is not a type of crossdocking?

    a. Manufacturing
    b. Vendor
    c. Distributor
    d. Retail
    e. Transportation
    f. Opportunistic

7. Which is an advantage of crossdocking?

    a. High visibility and control.
    b. Partnership with vendors.
    c. Reduced handling costs.
    d. Vendor cooperation.
    e. Strong quality control program for the inbound.

8. When structuring your logistics and supply chain network, every structure is a variant of the extremes of _____ and _____.

    a. Centralized, Decentralized
    b. Holding cost, Ordering cost
    c. Transportation, DCs
    d. Crossdocking, Architecture
    e. Metrics, Crossdocking

9. Which is not an advantage of centralization?

    a. Risk pooling
    b. Economies of scale
    c. Economies of scope
    d. Coordination advantages
    e. High visibility and control

10. Which is not something you use to develop a thorough organizational structure by balancing internal and external resources?

    a. Steering group
    b. Program management group

  c. Business change group

  d. Logistic group

  e. Project management group

  f. Project working group

11. What is in the center of change in business?

  a. People

  b. Transportation

  c. Money

  d. Manufacturing

  e. Failures

12. _____ have evolved out of the outsourcing trend of third-party service providers.

  a. 3PLs

  b. 4PLs

  c. Freight forwarding

  d. Project management

  e. International distribution

13. Country where two-thirds of the roads are unusable for modern trucks?

  a. Russia

  b. Japan

  c. United States

  d. China

  e. Taiwan

14. Which of the following are not among the drivers leading European companies toward integration of their physical distribution systems?

  a. Stockouts being more frequent.

  b. Profit levels failing to meet management objectives.

  c. Operational performance varying widely by brand, business, or unit.

d. Customer service levels not contributing to competitive differentiation.

e. Inventory levels high and rising higher with a poor demand–supply balance.

15. Which is not among the characteristics of facility networks that are more difficult to control?

    a. Several languages and cultures
    b. Labor norms
    c. Customs
    d. Infrastructure
    e. Freight rates

CHAPTER 6

Uncertainty

Global environment		
The supply chain	**Supply chain flows**	
Intercorporate coordination (functional shifting, third-party providers, relationship management, supply chain structures)	*Two-way flows*	
Marketing	⟵———⟶	
Sales	Products	
Research and development	Services	Customer satisfaction/
Forecasting	Information	value/
Production	Financial resources	profitability/
Purchasing		competitive
Logistics		advantage
Inventory management		
Information systems	*One-way flows*	
Finance	⟵ Demand	
Customer service	Forecasts ⟶	
Supplier's supplier ⟷ Supplier ⟷ Focal firm ⟷ Customer ⟷ Customer's customer		

(Left vertical label: Inter-functional coordination trust, commitment, risk, dependence, behaviors)

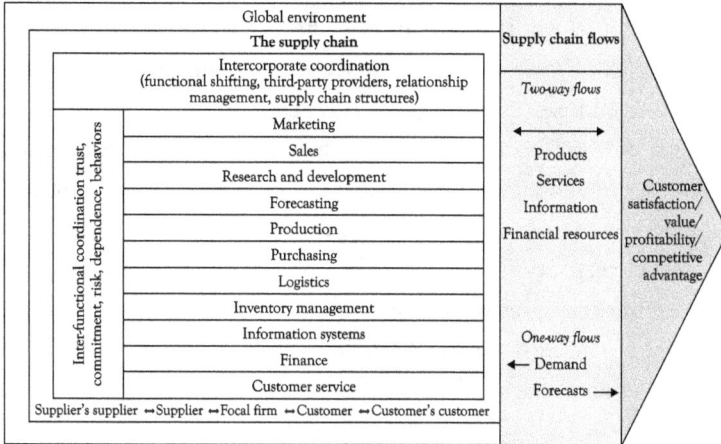

Chapter Objectives

- Expand on the impact of uncertainty in the supply chain as discussed in prior chapters
- Discuss the differences between demand side and supply side uncertainty
- Learn more about the bullwhip effect introduced in Chapter 4 (on forecasting)
- Consider coping strategies for SCM uncertainty
- Review mini-case examples of best practices

With today's move toward globalization, firms are managing increasingly complex supply chains of subsidiaries, customers, and suppliers. IT helps manage this complexity either by providing supply chain information, facilitating communication between supply chain partners, or supporting managers' decisions when coordinating these networks. As Kim and Oh (2000) put it, "global coordination is one of the most important functions firms have to perform for optimal global operations to achieve operational flexibility." Alliances, up- and downstream the supply chain often decide the success or failure of a firm. A basic requirement for a company participating in a supply chain is to open up their own information system for input from up- and downstream sources. Companies receive information from other members of the chain and disclose their own data to others. Unobstructed information flow, however, with all its positive implications, bears a huge potential of risk. Uncontrollable factors gain importance with the increase of a system's complexity and can occur unexpectedly. Data received may be misinterpreted and the biased information may be further distributed and amplified throughout the supply chain. As a consequence, long-term planning is extremely difficult and the enlargement of the time horizon increases uncertainty. The following section will describe certain sources of uncertainty and provide strategies of how to resolve these problems in an attempt to improve the supply chain to the benefit of all participants. The areas of emphasis will be:

- *Areas of uncertainty*
- *Coping strategies*
- *Supplier relationships*
- *Seamless supply chain*
- *Best practices*

Supply Chain Uncertainty

In order to cope with uncertainty within the supply chain, one must first understand and identify the sources within the various categories and between them. Using the Supply chain operations reference (SCOR) configurational model (see Figure 6.1), we can see that uncertainty and IT issues are not expressly listed.

In general, uncertainty can occur within each of the five categories as part of daily operations. Uncertainty can also exist *between* each of the categories. IT comes into play as a way of coordinating the various categories and reducing the uncertainty. One way of thinking about it is that IT becomes the arrows in the diagram.

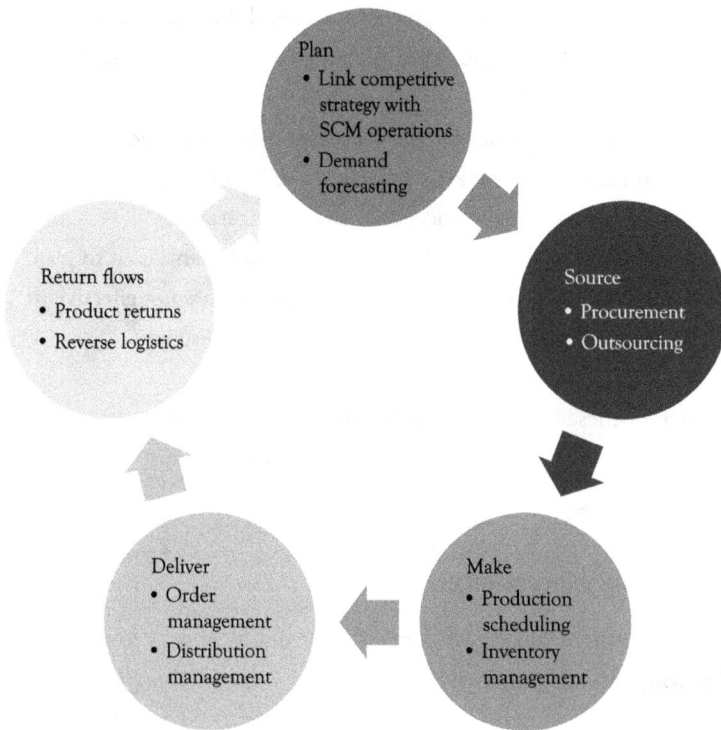

Figure 6.1 Operational categories of supply chain management

Now, if we wish to categorize the various sources of uncertainty that occur within the supply chain, they can be grouped in the following four areas:

- *Demand Side*: This source of uncertainty can be simply explained as the immediate customer. The company responds to the information obtained from the needs of the customers it supplies. As this information flows upstream throughout the various levels of the supply chain the accuracy of the data is distorted and less reliable.
- *Supply Side*: Materials, components, and subassemblies supplied by various vendors contribute to this source. Uncertainty stems from the large number of unpredictable possibilities that could disrupt the material flow from suppliers. A recent example is the September 11, 2001 terrorist

attack on the United States, which closed the U.S. borders causing JIT deliveries from Canadian and Mexican suppliers to be impossible.

- *Manufacturing Process:* This process consists of all the steps that the company takes to produce the final product. The lack of efficiency in this process can add to uncertainty.
- *Planning and Control Systems:* These are the systems used to plan and control the supply chain. If these systems are not effectively managed, they will also result in increased uncertainty.

Each of these sources of uncertainty leads to various problems in the supply chain. The types of problems are summarized in the following Table 6.1.

Demand Side Uncertainty

One of the main aspects of demand side uncertainty is known as the "**Bullwhip Effect**," otherwise known as the *amplification effect*, which is

Table 6.1 Problems with uncertainty

Uncertainty Source Affected	Cause of Uncertainty: Particular Weaknesses Observed in Real-World Value Stream
Process Side	• No measures of process performance • Reactive rather than proactive maintenance • Random shop floor layout • Interference between value streams
Supply Side	• Short notification of changes to supplier requirement • Excessive supplier delivery lead time • Adversarial supplier relationship • No vendor measures of performances
Demand Side	• No customer stock visibility • Adversarial customer relationship • Large infrequent deliveries to customer • Continuous product modifications causing high levels of obsolescence
Control Side	• Poor stock auditing • No synchronization and poor visibility among adjacent processes • Incorrect supplier lead time in MRP logic • Infrequent MRP runs

simply upstream order magnification. This means as information travels upstream in the supply chain, each level increases inventory causing forecasting data to have a nonuniform, increasing swinging motion, as shown in Figure 6.2. This causes data and material flow to become inefficient and distorted as you progress upstream in the process.

Throughout the different levels of the supply chain both information and material flow become distorted. This distortion causes the chain to become more and more inefficient as you progress upstream in the process.

Figure 6.2 outlines how each level in the supply chain adds a small amount of variance (uncertainty) in how they respond to the initial customer demand. By the time that the final orders have reached the production plant, they do not remotely reflect the actual customer demand pattern.

Forrester (1961) defined an information-feedback system as one that "exists when the environment leads to a decision that results in action, which affects the environment and thereby influences future decisions." He showed that this feedback mechanism led to an amplification or "bullwhip effect" that is a direct consequence of the dynamics and time-varying behaviors of any industrial organization.

In other words, the very forms and complex information systems structures required to manage a supply chain gives rise to undesirable behaviors (Lee et al. 1997). For example, signaling appropriate players of needed changes is difficult because the bullwhip effect creates inaccurate

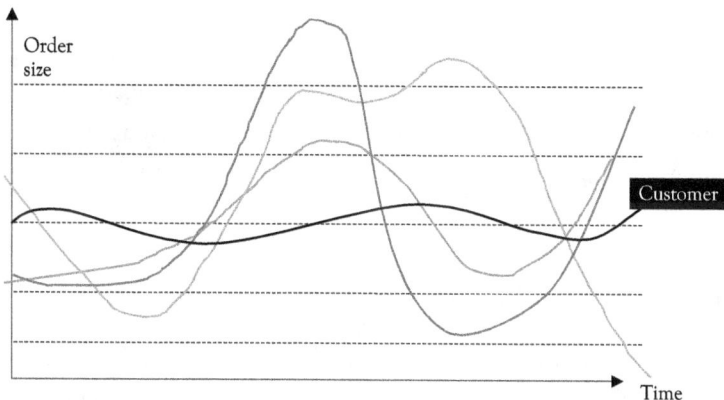

Figure 6.2 Bullwhip effect

forecast data, which is difficult to control (Taylor 2000). Translating appropriate data into desired forms also produces difficulties because the same basic data can lead to different measurements of the bullwhip effect, depending on the sequence of aggregating these data in the analysis.

What Are Possible Responses to Amplification Effects?

Information Sharing

One direct response is information sharing among all the members of the supply chain. Lee and Whang (1998) found that this information sharing should include sales data, order status (tracking data), sales forecasts, and production/delivery schedules. There is a critical relationship between partial and complete information sharing and inventory system performance.

If your supplier understands why your demand has fluctuated, they don't have to "guess," and when they "guess" they insert error into the system. This error escalates as the demand fluctuations ruminate throughout the supply chain—like ripples on a pond. One small rock can cause many ripples that get bigger the further they move away from the source. This is the essence of the bull-whip effect and demand side uncertainty.

Firms have attempted to integrate these various issues under the rubric of CPFR, in which all the firms in a supply chain share their inventory and forecasting data. CPFR, however, is a complex system which requires several specific actions at every step; this can be seen in the following Figure 6.3.

Firms such as Walmart and Dell have used CPFR to great advantage. Currently, the Voluntary Interindustry Commerce Standards (VICS) group provides a website listing best practices for CPFR along with information on implementation strategies. Information is available at www .vics.org/committees/cpfr/.

Utilize New Technology: Such as RFID

If trading partners use RFID it can provide visibility throughout the supply chain. This is another way that information sharing can occur. As we mentioned earlier, the key factor for widespread RFID tag usage is cost.

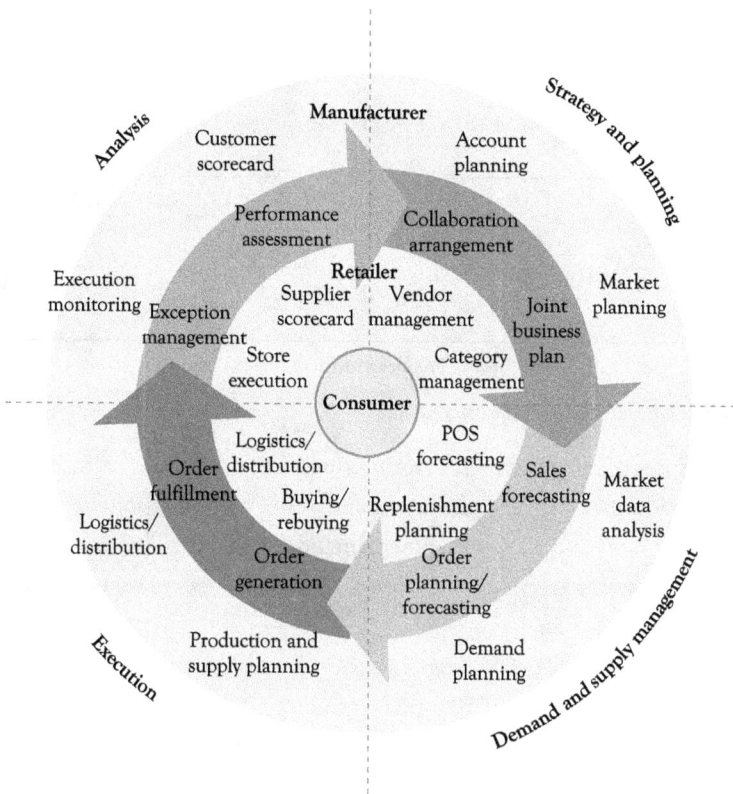

Figure 6.3 CPFR structure

Supply Side Uncertainty

Demand amplification or bullwhip effects are examples of serial interaction in the supply chain. In other words, a single customer and a single supplier interact between each tier of the supply chain. However, the supplier in each tier also interacts with other channels in the supply chain. These interactions within a single tier are known as parallel interactions and they can directly affect the traditional, serial interactions of a single supply chain.

As an example, Jones (1990) found parallel supply chain interactions within an automotive supply chain. Specifically, poor delivery performance and quality from some suppliers directly affected the efficiency of the good JIT suppliers. An example of how this can occur was provided by Wilding and Hill (1999) and can be seen in Figure 6.4.

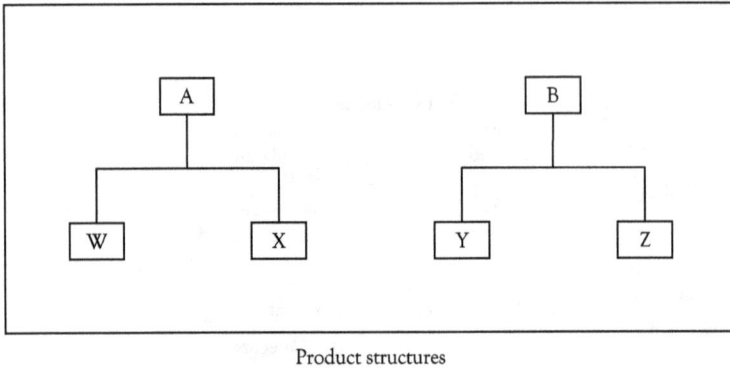

Product structures

Figure 6.4 Product structures

Assume a company builds two products, A and B, each requiring the same amount of capacity allocation and being composed of subcomponents W, X, Y, and Z. Assume the demand is 100 units and component part safety stocks are 50 units. As long as JIT deliveries are kept, the entire process remains stable.

What if part W is not delivered timely? In all likelihood, the manager will use the safety stock of 50 units to produce 50 units of A. After that, in an effort to keep capacity utilization high, the manager will use the spare capacity to produce 50 extra units of B. Assuming the delayed parts appear the next time period, the process will be reversed, and 50 extra units of A will be produced. Thus, at this level, production quickly goes back to equilibrium but the effects on the subsuppliers will take longer to stabilize. The consequences are similar to those of amplification effects and are as follows:

- Suppliers that provide good service and delivery will suffer disruption to their schedules due to suppliers that do not provide their level of service.
- Disruption of planned schedules remote from first-tier suppliers can be caused by changes in product mix.
- Customers are frequently unaware of the problems they create for suppliers by small schedule changes.

Concerning parallel uncertainty, Wilding (1998) found that suppliers and assemblers can either have their production stopped or their schedule disrupted by parallel interactions up to 18 percent of the time.

What Are the Possible Responses to Parallel Uncertainty Effects?

Intuition would suggest and research and practice has shown that parallel interactions can be reduced by increasing the amount of inventory in the supply chain. But wait, we don't want more inventory in the system, right? The goal of SCM is to minimize the inventory within the pipeline. Additionally, increasing inventories increases the amount of amplification uncertainty in the supply chain.

Unforeseen, nonlinear events are also an area of uncertainty in the supply chain. There are a range of events that may occur where some are minor and which are easy to adapt or events that are more profound. These more profound events are also known as "Black Swan" or "major nonlinear" events. These events are typically considered to happen rarely but create large disruptions in the supply chain leading to higher levels of uncertainty. A variety of these events may come about:

- Geopolitical unrest
- Spread of disease
- Natural disasters
- Technology failures

What Are Some Possible Responses to Uncertainty Due to Unforeseen Events?

Unforeseen events often come unexpectedly and without warning. To reduce uncertainty, methods such as scenario planning and testing may be used. Scenario planning can be implemented on a ranged system where the best and worst outcomes are determined. The supply chain is then tested on these scenarios to determine how the supply chain would react. This reduces uncertainty by allowing preparation for these events. Seamless communication with technology integration through an IT system could also be used to mitigate risk and uncertainty. A firm that employs this method would be able to react quickly to major disruptions. This method will be explained further in the chapter involving planning and control systems.

Here again we see that the role of SCM is complex, yet critical to the organization. Trade-offs must be analyzed and considered in light of your business goals, strategy, processes, suppliers, and customers.

Manufacturing Process Uncertainty

Within the manufacturing system, there are numerous areas of uncertainty associated with the various manufacturing processes. One example is the use of MRP systems and the problem of limited planning horizons (which is why MRP systems are frozen after certain time periods).

Four distinct areas have been identified where manufacturing issues can cause uncertainty and actually exasperate the amplification or bullwhip effect (Lee et al. 1997):

- **Demand forecast updating**, where increasing safety stock in the pipeline causes erroneous amplification of demand in the supply chain.
- **Order batching**, where customers tend to order goods during particular times. For example, the manufacturer may get large bulk orders followed by long periods of low demand based on changing order patterns from its customers. Communication is key to understanding the changes.
- **Price fluctuations**, where promotions and "loss leaders" cause surges in demand. This is caused by customers buying more product sooner than they usually would (this is referred to as forward buying).
- **Rationing and shortage gaming**, where retailers submit multiple orders when supply is scarce. The idea is that by submitting multiple orders above their actual requirements, they will receive what they actually need. If the manufacturer doesn't know what is happening, this seeming increase to demand will affect its future forecasts and potentially cause overstocking.

What Are the Possible Responses to Manufacturing Process Uncertainty Effects?

Each of these effects can be resolved through communication. First, the anomaly in ordering patterns, consumption, and so on must be identified. Once the change is identified, the responsible manager can investigate and inquire as to the causes. The primary goal for the manager is first to implement internal control mechanisms to identify changes, such as some sort of statistical process control as is used in quality management. If the issue is not identified, it cannot be isolated and investigated. The change should not be assumed, normal course of business, without first ensuring that is truly the case.

It is a common occurrence, in our experience, that fluctuations in demand due to promotions are not systematically tracked. This causes future forecasts to be erroneous. For example, let's consider a consumer products manufacturer who agrees to run a promotion in conjunction with a customer in the Spring of 2012. This promotion causes demand for the promotional product to be increased above normal demand. If this promotional activity is not captured systematically, it will erroneously increase the forecast for that item in the next period, or even as far out as the Spring of 2013.

Planning and Control Systems

Although huge amounts of money have been spent on IT to coordinate the various members of supply chains, the technology has its limitations. One of the fallacies of traditional long-term planning and forecasting and its traditional modeling tools is that they are incapable of predicting discontinuities (i.e., major nonlinearities, an extreme example being the 9/11 attacks) (Mintzberg 1994). While certain repetitive or seasonal patterns may be easily predictable, other issues such as technological innovations or price increases are not.

Uncertainty has been differentiated into four levels (Courtney et al. 1997):

- A clear-enough future
- Alternative future
- A range of futures
- True ambiguity

Various types of uncertainties impact the planning forecast at each of these four uncertainty levels. For example, if incorrect data is being represented, then this impacts the robustness of any of the tool sets being used to solve a problem. Overall, these uncertainties interact to such a point that a long-range forecast/model in the "range of futures" or "total ambiguity" stage can become nothing more than a "gut instinct" call on the part of the decision maker. This is not to say that this type of forecasting is unforgivable, it is simply a reality and falls under the category of qualitative forecasting that we mentioned earlier.

Coping Strategies for Supply Chain Uncertainty

In the previous section, we provided some basic strategies for responding to specific types of uncertainty. In this section, we delve deeper into methods of responding to uncertainty. Specifically, those that focus on the supply chain as a whole. This framework can be seen in Figures 6.5 and 6.6.

The general mode of attack is to address these issues in this order:

1. *Manufacturing process and supply side*

   ○ Implement "Lean Thinking" into the manufacturing process. Lean thinking is a concept that deals with eliminating all the waste and inefficiency within a process.

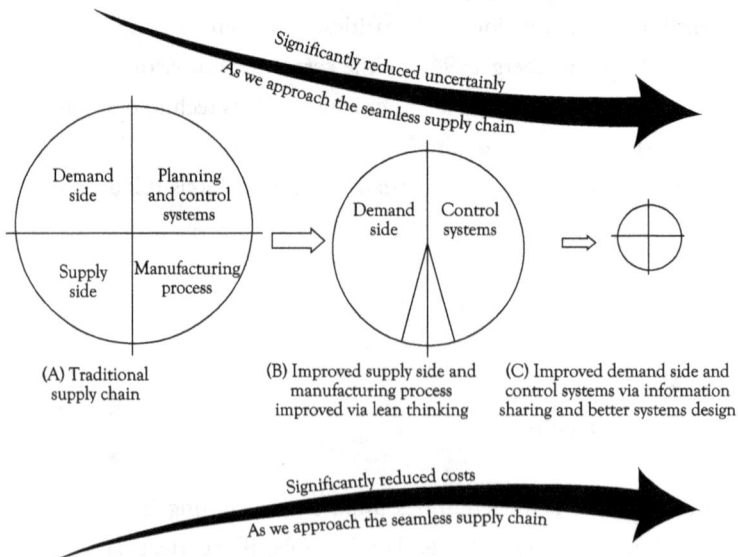

Figure 6.5 Uncertainty coping strategies

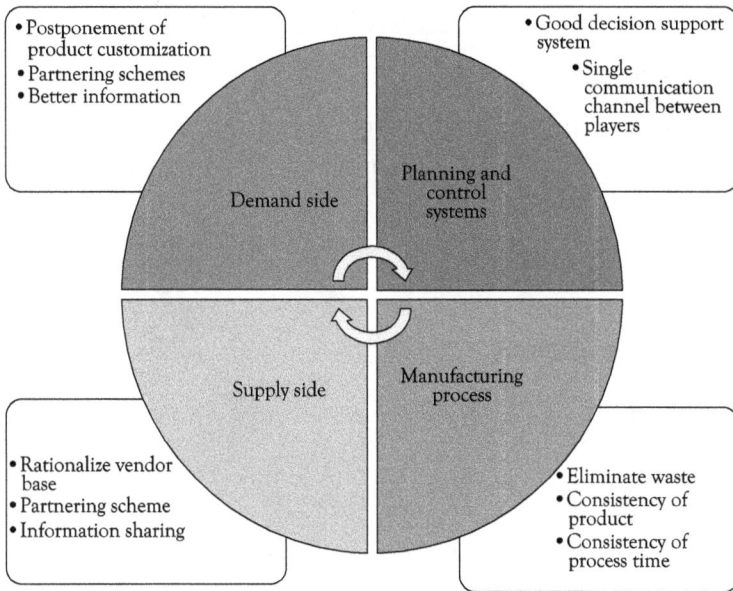

Figure 6.6 Final issues in coping with uncertainty

    ○ Continuously improve relationships with suppliers. The goal is to integrate them into the supply chain so that they know exactly what you need from them to be successful together.

2. *Demand side and control systems*

    ○ Information sharing is key. The best strategy is to use one method of communication with suppliers and allow them direct access to consumer information. This will enable them to be proactive rather than reactive. This will also add value to the overall supply chain and reduce the magnitude of the "Bullwhip Effect." There must be a system in place with timely accurate information available for planning and decision making.

    ○ Address interdepartmental coordination. Ensure that internal information flows are planned, expected, and working properly. Do not make the mistake of assuming that the "left hand knows what the right hand is doing." Get out of your office and see for yourself that everyone is working from the same game plan.

Cost Benefit Analysis of "Lean Thinking"

Although the goal of an efficient supply chain is to run in a lean manner to reduce cost and waste, it must be considered with the uncertainty and risk involved in running a lean system.

A lean supply chain:

- Improves efficiency
- Reduces waste
- Creates innovation and quality

However, a disruptive event may cause:

- Stock outs
- Lost sales
- Amplification effect of all firms involved
- Decreased value of firm due to competition
- Decreased market-share due to competition

A lean supply chain provides an advantage that creates more efficiency and quality in a process; however, these benefits must be weighed with the risks. A supply chain that is unprepared for a disruptive event due to lean thinking can have serious consequences for the firm.

Analyses can be applied on the overall risk of the supply chain involving lean thinking through a variety of variables such as:

- Diversity of suppliers
- Level of technology and data flow
- Supplier relationships
- Skill of supply chain managers to adapt

A firm must weigh the risk of a lean or JIT system with uncertainty in order to create the best operational model for the firm's supply chain.

Supply Chain Partnerships

Uncertainty in the supply chain impacts the performance of all the trading partners up and down the chain. To cope with such uncertainties in the supply chain firms can create an alliance with its suppliers. As discussed earlier, firms can attain their competitive advantage by working closely with their suppliers.

Traditionally, American and European firms have been using a large pool of suppliers to increase their bargaining power in terms of lower costs, higher quality, and faster delivery times. In recent times, firms have focused on reducing the supplier base since the close association with specific suppliers can lead to relationship-based discounts. Most of these trends toward a smaller supplier base have been fueled by the success of Japanese firms that recognize the strategic buyer–supplier partnerships as a critical factor for success.

The benefits of partnerships to buyer firms in the form of lower cost and higher quality have been widely cited in the literature. Generally, there is a notion that suppliers lose out in partnerships with buyers. Suppliers, however, also benefit from adopting the strategy of maintaining partnerships with the buyer firms as compared to using a transactional approach to servicing customers. A list of the benefits of supplier relationships is summarized in Table 6.2.

Table 6.2 Benefits of supplier partnerships (Adapted from Maloni and Benton 1997)

Benefits For Buyers	Cost Savings
Cost Quantity Discounts High quality Improved timing	Economies of scale Ordering Production Transportation
Benefits For Suppliers	
Market Understanding of customer needs	Administrative Switching Process integration
Benefits For Both	
Convergent expectation and goals Reduced effects from externalities Reduced Opportunism	Joint products and process development Improved communication Shared risk and rewards

Reducing Uncertainty Through Supplier Diversification

In the supply chain, supplier relationships are extremely important to ensuring that the supply chain operates at a high rate of efficiency and that the best outcomes are being developed overall. Although having few suppliers in which close relationships can be built brings benefits such as better prices, better communication, and efficiency, it does not reduce the uncertainty of the supply chain as much as it should. When only a few suppliers are used, the uncertainty and risk of the supply chain will increase. This is due to less options of procuring inventory and materials when a disruptive event occurs, such as Covid-19.

Over the years, China has become a major hub of manufacturing various goods for many firms globally. This has led to China being a leading manufacturer of goods of everything from clothing, electronic components, car components, and household goods. With the Covid-19 pandemic originating in China, many firms' supply chains were disrupted due to a large slowdown of manufacturing activity within the country. To reduce supply chain risk, a firm must have a diversity of suppliers in which to procure products and materials in the event of a disruption. Although it may produce higher costs, it may reduce the overall cost by preventing lost sales due to the lack of inventory and delays.

Lean Thinking and Supplier Diversification

Supplier diversification plays an important role in the idea of lean thinking in a supply chain. Supply chain diversification can be used to determine the level of uncertainty and risk to determine the best level of lean operation.

To determine the best method for a lean supply chain, risk and uncertainty can be determined by an analysis of supplier diversification and location. A supply chain that has a few suppliers located near each other creates the highest level of risk regarding these variables. Therefore, caution should be taken in developing a lean strategy for this supply chain. Since a localized event could cause a disruption in the supplier operations, it creates a need for a less lean supply chain. A firm with a supply chain in this case should maintain a higher level of safety stock to reduce the uncertainty and risk. A firm with a supply chain that has a larger number of suppliers that are more dispersed globally has a lower uncertainty and risk. Therefore, such a firm may choose to operate on a leaner system.

A firm should assess their uncertainty and risk based on the number and location of their suppliers. This will create a better picture of the overall uncertainty and risk to the firm's supply chain.

As we have discussed previously, forming a partnership is not an easy task since it requires a significant attitudinal as well as structural change on the part of both partners. Selecting the right partner from a pool of alternatives is a challenging task, which requires considering the issues of compatibility in terms of culture and management styles. Sustaining a supply chain partnership requires a fair amount of cooperation, trust, and goodwill between the partners. When cooperation, trust, and goodwill is there, however, you can work together to form a seamless supply chain (Table 6.2).

The Seamless Supply Chain

Achieving world-class delivery precision is one of the most demanding and challenging goals of customer-oriented end producers and their suppliers. Designing and operating efficient supply chains are major requirements for delivery precision. Common wisdom holds that the markets will force companies to build and operate highly efficient supply chains, but the entire supply chain is important—not just an individual company. The seamless supply chain is a perfect flow of information and materials facilitated by all supply chain partners. This supply chain can only be reached by reducing sources of uncertainty throughout the extended supply chain. Today, people expend significant effort to expedite orders, check order status frequently, deploy inventory, "just in case" pad lead times, or find other creative ways to buffer themselves against disruptive events. A recent survey on SCM issues showed that nearly 40 percent of the surveyed companies are currently preparing to implement various SCM tools and technology. But fewer than 10 percent of them have actually implemented smooth material flow principles and have productive solutions in place.

There is a strong relationship between the best-in-class supply chain practices and levels of supply chain uncertainty. The following is the summary of closely related best practices:

- *Simplicity:* This involves the adoption of the already proven solutions such as inventory reduction, simplified products and processes, flexibility, and commitment to continuous and incremental improvement.
- *Smooth material flow:* To establish a smooth material flow along the value stream so that a product proceeds from design to launch, from order to delivery and from raw materials to a finished product in the hands of the customer with no stoppages, scrap, or backflows.
- *Value stream management:* This makes sure that products move in a more effective fashion, from concept to launch, from order to delivery, and from sourcing of raw materials to delivery to the customer.
- *Lean thinking:* As discussed, this is a philosophy that seeks to shorten the time between customer order and product delivery by eliminating sources of waste and delay.

Of course, by virtue of the fact that these are best practices, most firms are not performing at this level. So how does a supply chain manager assess how close they are to these best practices and whether they are making progress? One way is to determine what stage of supply chain maturity they are at and with it, how well they can manage uncertainty.

Stages of Supply Chain Maturity and Uncertainty

The Stevens reference framework divides supply chain evolution into four levels:

- **Level One (Baseline):** Companies engage in reactive short-term planning and "firefighting." They have large pools of inventory and are vulnerable to market changes.

- **Level Two (Functional Integration):** Companies focus inward on goods and are reactive toward their customers.
- **Level Three (Internal Integration):** All work processes are integrated and the planning process reaches from the customers back to the supplier.
- **Level Four (External Integration):** The organization achieves integration with all suppliers and synchronizes material flows to form an extended enterprise.

Once a company has determined its stage of supply chain integration and the type of uncertainty to be reduced, it should look for the causes of uncertainty. The process of supply chain reengineering continues until external integration and best-in-class status is reached. The result is a plan taken by the best firms. The plan lays out the steps that a typical company would take in improving its supply chain operations.

Benefits of Reducing Uncertainty

- Increased visibility
- Remove operational drag
- Improve performance of an organization
- Decrease cost
- Increase market share and profitability
- Reduce inventory

Figure 6.7 shows how the adoption of best practices leads to a reduction in the supply chain uncertainty and this in turn results in a more integrated supply chain. At each level of supply chain integration, the different types of uncertainty are reduced; however, uncertainty can never be eliminated.

Mini-Case: Best Practices

Digital equipment—to squash competition from direct vendors and expand *Seamless Supply Chain* used a final assembly model to lower the

Stage of Supply Chain Integration	Stage of Supply Chain Integration	Relative Uncertainty Quantities			
		Process	Supply	Control	Demand
1. Baseline	Reactive short-term planning. Firefighting. Large pools of inventory. Vulnerability to market changes.	4	4	4	4
2. Functional Integration	Emphasis still on cost, not performance. Focus inward and on goods. Reactive toward customer. Some internal trade-offs.	2	4	3	4
3. Internal Integration	All work processes integrated. Planning reaches from customer back to supplier. EDI widely used. Still reacting to customer.	1	2	2	4
4. External Integration	Integration of all suppliers. Focus on customer. Synchronized material flows. SC covers extended enterprise.	1	1	1	1

Figure 6.7 Benchmarking uncertainty management

total *supply chain* cost, improve product delivery time, with flexibility in obtaining customized PCs.

Although the base systems and core components owned by Digital will sit in Hall-Mark's warehouse until an order is received, the units will be "kitted" to sport the exact hardware options sought by a reseller. Once assembled, the PCs will be tested and loaded with the factory-installed software. This is an instance of process uncertainty fix with value- added warehouses. A Digital-employed asset manager will ensure that each system is suitable for sale. In exchange for this work, Digital will pay Hall-Mark an undisclosed assembly fee. Hall-Mark officials say this program will better position its resellers to meet customer needs such as building to users' specifications and turning around an order within a day's time.

Cisco's model of building a seamless supply chain is one that many companies can follow. It proves that you do not have to own or control most of the elements in your supply chain, yet have complete visibility of the chain. The Internet allows companies to coordinate more closely with their suppliers and also enables JIT delivery that lets businesses greatly reduce inventories. Cisco's suppliers build and ship while Cisco handles all of the financial transactions. This is an excellent instance of control/demand uncertainty fix.

Ford and its suppliers are following Cisco's lead for reduced inventories, inefficiencies, faster transactions, and shorter order to payment cycles. Ford is giving its suppliers greater responsibility for building whole modules to be assembled in finished cars. Ford's push to e-business is to trigger mass customization where a customer configures his car through the company's website with greater brand choices. Also, supply chains are being built within the supply chain where suppliers and customers are reaping benefits alike. This is an instance of demand/supply uncertainty fix.

Dell is another instance where all the hardware/software can be configured online. Vendors manage the inventories while Dell only builds the final assembly and has strategically placed its suppliers close to its geographical proximity to avoid delays.

Italian clothes manufacturer, *Benetton*, used postponement as its strategy to buffer for color demand uncertainty. With an IT-integrated supply chain, capturing point of sale (POS) data, the mainframe in Italy knew instantly what the demand at any time was. It had its yarn knitted into sweaters and postponed the process of dyeing until it received the order. Thus, it could ship the orders to customers within three weeks.

Target in adapting to Covid-19. Target was able to gain market share in online sales. Using their retail stores as fulfillment centers, they increased utilization of the store fronts in a time where foot traffic was lower. They benefited from 2 million new user orders for store pickup.

Key Takeaways

- Supply chain uncertainty can be broken into four categories: demand side, supply side, manufacturing processes, and planning and control systems. Breaking down uncertainty into categories allows you to understand the sources generating the uncertainty and allow you to address it systematically and proactively.
- The bullwhip effect is a significant contributor to supply chain uncertainty. Strategic information sharing with suppliers and customers can allow the firm to control the variability associated with this amplification of errors within the supply chain.
- There are coping strategies that allow companies to address uncertainty and its effects. These include, but are not limited

to, lean thinking, building relationships with suppliers, information sharing throughout the value chain, and improving interdepartmental coordination.

- Best practices to address supply chain uncertainty include simplicity, smooth material flow, value stream management, and lean thinking.

Reflection Points

1. What other benefits, besides those mentioned in this chapter, would your company reap if uncertainty is reduced within your supply chain? Any uncertainty within your supply chain affects many other aspects of your company's health and vitality—what health benefits do you foresee for support functions within your organization if uncertainty is reduced in the supply chain? These types of benefits, those that affect the support systems within organizations are often forgotten. Be sure to consider them when weighing options.

2. When you think about the uncertainty experienced by your company—is it primarily externally or internally generated? Do you have processes in place to differentiate between the two?

3. What can you and/or your team do to address each of the best practices mentioned? Which of these four do you believe is the most important to reducing uncertainty within your supply chain? Why? Can you think of any "low hanging fruit" that you could address and get a quick win in this arena?

4. What proactive steps can you take in order to address known or unknown uncertainty that is outside of your company but within your supply chain? How many steps or tiers in your supply chain do you believe should be addressed? Have you considered teaming with companies such as DHL 360 Resilience to help you manage this type of uncertainty?

Additional Resources

Davis, T. Summer 1993. "Effective Supply Chain Management." Sloan Management Review, pp. 35–46.

De Meyer, A., C.H. Loch, and M.T. Pich. Winter 2002. "Managing Project Uncertainty: From Variation to Chaos." MIT Sloan Management Review, pp. 60–67.

Dhillon, G. and J. Ward. 2002. "Chaos Theory as a Framework for Studying Information Systems." Information Resources Management Journal 15, no. 2, pp. 5–13.

Diehl, E. and J.D. Sterman. 1995. "Effects of Feedback Complexity on Dynamic Decision-Making." Organizational Behavior and Human Decision Processes 62, no. 2, pp. 198–215.

Donovan, J. 2003. "RF Identification Tags: Show Me the Money." Electronic Engineering Times, p. 41.

Duris, R. September 2003. "The Seven Deadly Sins of Supply Chain Management." *Frontline Solutions.*

Egelhoff, W.G. 1991. "Information-Processing Theory and the Multinational Enterprise." Journal of International Business Studies 22, no. 3, pp. 341–369.

Eisenhardt, K.M. Winter 2002. "Has Strategy Changed." *MIT Sloan Management Review.*

Elllis, S. and S. Lambright. 2002. "Real Time Tech—Unilever Sees Intelligent Product Tags as the Brains Behind Real-Time Supply Chains." Optimize, p. 44.

Fernie, J. 1994. "Quick Response: An International Perspective." International Journal of Physical Distribution and Logistics Management 24, no. 6, pp. 38–46.

Finkenzeller, K. 1999. RFID Handbook. Chichester, UK: John Wiley & Sons.

Fisher, M.L. 1997. "What Is the Right Supply Chain for Your Product?" *Harvard Business Review* 75, no. 2, pp. 105–17.

Forrester. 1961. Industrial Dynamics. Cambridge, MA: MIT Press.

Geary, S., P. Childerhouse, and D.R. Towill. July/August 2002. "Uncertainty and the Seamless Supply Chain." Supply Chain Management Review, pp. 52–59.

Gilliland, M. and D. Prince. 2001. "New Approaches to 'Unforecastable' Demand." Journal of Business Forecasting Methods and Systems 20, no. 2, pp. 9–13.

Gould, L.S. 2000. "What You Need to Know About RFID." Automotive Manufacturing and Production 112, no. 2, pp. 46–49.

Gregerson, H. and L. Sailor. 1993. "Chaos Theory and Its Implications for Social Science Research." Human Relations 46, no. 7, pp. 777–802.

Ho, C. 1992. "An Examination of a Distribution Resource Planning Problem: DRP Systems Nervousness." Journal of Business Logistics 13, no. 2, pp. 125–152.

Hogarth, R. and S. Makridakis. 1981. "The Value of Decision-Making in a Complex Environment: An Experimental Approach." Management Science 27, no. 1, pp. 93–107.

Karkkainen, M. and J. Holmstrom. 2002. "Wireless Product Identification: Enabler for Handling Efficiency, Customisation and Information Sharing." Supply Chain Management: An International Journal 7, no. 4, pp. 242–252.

Kim, B. and H. Oh. 2000. "An Exploratory Inquiry Into the Perceived Effectiveness of a Global Information System." *Information Management and Computer Security 8*, no. 3, pp. 144–153.

Kunii, I.M. October 20, 2003. "Radio ID Tags So Cheap They'll Be Everywhere." BusinessWeek, p. 147.

Lee, H.L. 2002. "Aligning Supply Chain Strategies With Product Uncertainties." *California Management Review 44*, no. 3, pp. 105–119.

Lee, H.L. and S. Whang. 1998. Information Sharing in a Supply Chain. Stanford, Graduate School of Business, Stanford University.

Lee, H.L., V. Padmanabhan, and S. Whang. 1997. "Information Distortion in a Supply Chain: The Bullwhip Effect." Management Science 43, no. 4, pp. 546–558.

Lee, H.L., V. Padmanabhan, and S. Whang. 1997. "The Bullwhip Effect in Supply Chains." Sloan Management Review, pp. 93–102.

Levy, D. Summer 1994. "Chaos Theory and Strategy: Theory, Application and Managerial Implications." Strategic Management Journal 15, pp. 167–178.

MacMillan, I.C., A.B. Van Putten, and R.G. McGrath. May 2003. "Global Gamesmanship." *Harvard Business Review.*

Maloni, M.J. and W.C. Benton. 1997. "Supply Chain Partnerships: Opportunities for Operations Research." *European Journal of Operational Research* 101, no. 3, pp. 419–429.

Mason-Jones, R. and D.R. Towill. 2000. "Coping With Uncertainty: Reducing 'Bullwhip' Behavior in Global Supply Chains." *Supply Chain Forum* 1, pp. 40–45.

McGuffog, T. 1997. "Effective Management of the UK Value Chain." In Proceedings of the 1997 Logistics Research Network Conference. UK: Institute of Logistics.

Mintzberg, H. 1994. "Rethinking Strategic Planning Part I: Pitfalls and Fallacies." Long Range Planning 27, pp. 12–21.

Murray, C.J. 2003. "Emerging Markets–"Smart" Data Sets." Electronic Engineering Times, p. 38.

Nassauer, S. 2020. *Target Gains Strength During Coronavirus.* WSJ (April 30, 2021).

New, S. October 2010. "The Transparent Supply Chain." *Harvard Business Review* 88, no. 10, pp. 76–82.

Niemeyer, A., M.H. Pak, and S.E. Ramaswamy. 2003. "Smart Tags for Your Supply Chain." The McKinsey Quarterly 4.

Pagell, M. and C. Sheu. 2001. "Buyer Behaviours and the Performance of the Supply Chain: An International Exploration." *International Journal of Production Research* 39, no. 13, pp. 2783–2801.

Parker, D. 1994. Chaos Theory and the Management of Change. Birmingham, UK: Research Center for Industrial Strategy, University of Birmingham. Referenced in Wilding, R.D. 1998. Chaos Theory: Implications for Supply Chain Management.

Partch, K. July 15, 2000. "Is the Supermarket ERA at an End?" Supermarket Business 55, p. 138.

Priesmeyer, H.R. and J. Davis. Fall 1991. "Chaos Theory: A Tool for Predicting the Unpredictable." Journal of Business Forecasting, pp. 22–28.

Richardson, H.L. April 4, 2004. "Execution at the Dock." *Logistics Today.*

Salmon, K. 1993. Efficient Consumer Response: Enhancing Consumer Value in the Supply Chain. Washington, DC: Kurt Salmon.

Schaer, B. 1997. "Implementing a Crossdocking Operation." *IIESolutions,* pp. 34–36.

Schuster, E. 2004. The Future With Auto-ID Technology. APICS Webinar.

Shore, B. 2001. "Information Sharing in Global Supply Chain Systems." Journal of Global Information Technology Management 4, no. 3, pp. 27–50.

Stacy, R. D. 1993. Strategic Management and Organizational Dynamics. London: Pittman.

Stalk, G., P. Evans, and L.E. Shulman. 1992. "Competing on Capabilities: The New Rules of Corporate Strategy." *Harvard Business Review,* pp. 57–69.

Stank, T., M. Crum, and M. Arango. 1999. "Benefits of Interfirm Coordination in Food Industry Supply Chains." Journal of Business Logistics 20, no. 2, pp. 21–41.

Stank, T.P. 1997. "Just-In-Time Management and Transportation Service Performance in a Cross-border Setting." Transportation Journal 36, no. 3, pp. 31–42.

Sterman, J.D. 1989. "Modeling Managerial Behavior: Misperceptions of Feedback in a Dynamic Decisions Making Experiment." Management Science 35, no. 3, pp. 321–339.

Sterman, J.D. 2001. "System Dynamics Modeling: Tools for Learning in a Complex World." California Management Review 43, no. 4, pp. 8–25.

Stock, G.N., N.P. Greis, and J.D. Kasarda. 2000. "Enterprise Logistics and Supply Chain Structure: The Role of Fit." Journal of Operations Management 18, pp. 531–547.

Strogatz, S. 2003. SYNC: The Emerging Science of Spontaneous Order. New York, NY: Hyperion.

Swenseth, S.R. and F.P. Buffa. 1991. "Implications of Inbound Lead Time Variability for Just-In-Time Manufacturing." International Journal of Operations and Production Management 11, no. 7, pp. 37–48.

Taylor, D.H. 2000. "Demand Amplification: Has It Got Us Beat?" International Journal of Physical Distribution and Logistics Management 30, no. 6, pp. 515–533.

Thomas, C. and L. Tom. December 2011. *"Don't Let Your Supply Chain Control Your Business." Harvard Business Review* 89, no. 12, pp. 112–117.

Van der Horst, J.G.A.J. and A.J.M. Beulens. 2002. "Identifying Sources of Uncertainty to Generate Supply Chain Redesign Strategies." *International Journal of Physical Distribution and Logistics Management* 32, no. 6, pp. 409–430.

Vidal, C.J. and M. Goetschalckx. 2000. "Modeling the Effect of Uncertainties on Global Logistics Systems." Journal of Business Logistics 21, no. 1, pp. 95–121.

Walden, M. 1996. Journal of Business Forecasting 15, no. 2.

Wilding, R.D. 1997. "An Investigation Into Sources of Uncertainty Within Industrial Supply Chains: Amplification, Deterministic Chaos, and Parallel Interactions." Engineering Department. Warwick, Coventry, UK: University of Warwick.

Wilding, R.D. 1998. "Chaos Theory: Implications for Supply Chain Management." The International Journal of Logistics Management 9, no. 1, pp. 43–56.

Wilding, R.D. 1998. "The Supply Chain Complexity Triangle: Uncertainty Generation in the Supply Chain." International Journal of Physical Distribution and Logistics Management 28, no. 8, pp. 599–616.

Wilding, R.D. and J.F. Hill. 1999. "Parallel Interactions in Supply Chains." In 2nd International Symposium on Advanced Manufacturing Processes, Systems and Technologies. AMPST 99.

Zwolinski, K. 2003. "Changing Supplies." *Manufacturing Engineer,* pp. 14–17.

Multiple Choice Questions

1. According to Kim and Oh, _____ is one of the most important functions firms have to perform for optimal global operations to achieve operational flexibility.

   a. Global coordination

   b. Interdepartmental coordination

   c. Uncertainty preparation

   d. Risk management

   e. Production planning/Forecasting

2. Which of the following is not an operational category of supply chain management?

a. Plan
b. Make
c. Source
d. Marketing
e. Deliver

3. Which of the following is not a source of uncertainty in the supply chain?

a. Supply side
b. Demand side
c. Intercompany collaboration
d. Manufacturing process
e. Planning and control systems

4. What term best describes upstream order magnification?

a. Lean manufacturing
b. The bullwhip effect
c. Risk mitigation
d. Vendor-managed inventory
e. CPFR

5. What is not one of the benefits of reducing uncertainty?

a. Increased inventory
b. Increased visibility
c. Improved performance of an organization
d. Decreased costs
e. Increased market share and profitability

6. What is not a best practice to address uncertainty in the supply chain?

a. Simplicity
b. Smooth material flow
c. Value stream management
d. Lean thinking
e. Increased inventories

7. What best describes company inventory that is tracked and main-tained by a supplier, instead of the buying company?

   a. RFID
   b. VMI
   c. The bullwhip effect
   d. CPFR
   e. VIS

8. What is not an example of a nonlinear event?

   a. White swan events
   b. Geopolitical unrest
   c. Spread of disease
   d. Natural disasters
   e. Technology failures

9. What best describes creating a range of outcomes, from worst to best, then testing the supply chain to determine how it will be affected?

   a. Artificial intelligence
   b. Capacity planning
   c. Scenario planning
   d. Disaster control
   e. Forecasting

10. Customers that have _____ suppliers that are _____ each other have increased risk and uncertainty.

   a. Fewer; further from
   b. More; further from
   c. More; near
   d. Fewer; near
   e. Fewer; related to

11. What is used to help manage the increasingly complex supply chains of subsidiaries, customers and suppliers?

   a. Scenario planning
   b. VMI

c. Information Technology (IT)

d. White swan events

e. Supplier relationships

12. Which system led to the amplification of the bullwhip effect?

a. VMI

b. CPFR

c. Demand forecast updating

d. Information feedback

e. Information sharing

13. Which of the following topics is not included in the SCOR model?

a. Check

b. Plan

c. Source

d. Make

e. Deliver

14. The concept that deals with eliminating all the waste and inefficiency within a process?

a. Demand forecasting

b. Lean thinking

c. Capacity planning

d. Bullwhip effect

e. Seamless supply chain

15. Which company used postponement as its strategy to buffer for color demand uncertainty?

a. Ford

b. Target

c. Benetton

d. Dell

e. Cisco

CHAPTER 7

Information Technology

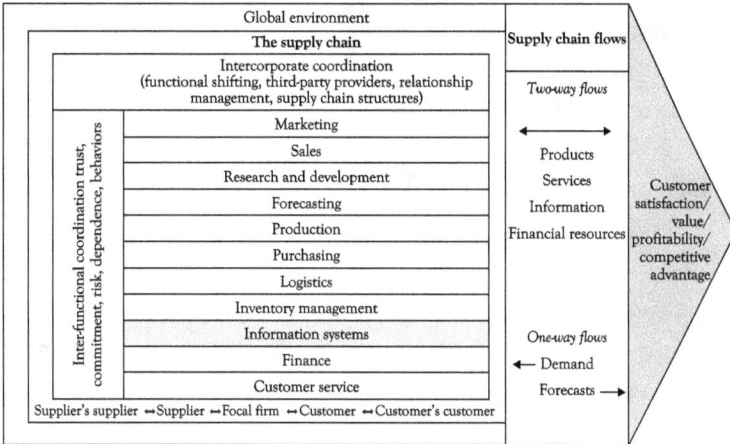

Chapter Objectives

- Introduce IT as it exists today
- Explore the goals of IT and SCM
- Discuss different types of IT solutions in SCM
- Explore the advantages and difficulties associated with IT in SCM
- Consider trends and implementation issues in IT
- Apply IT issues through mini-cases

The business environment is changing and the need for reducing uncertainty related to demand, supply, distance, and delivery time has been the focus of companies. This, coupled with an increasing need to manage activities, has necessitated the implementation of various ITs to reduce uncertainty such as the bullwhip effect and to improve coordination and synchronization. To address these issues, several IT solutions are used at various levels of the supply chain.

- *Upstream Supply Chain*: EDI, extranets, and virtual private networks.
- *Internal Supply Chain*: Intranets, data warehouse, ERP, MRP (I and II), traditional transaction processing systems, and executive information systems.
- *Downstream Supply Chain*: Customer relationship management (CRM), order management system, web services.

There are certain important developments that need to be focused on for successful IT-enabled SCM. These are as follows:

- *Strategic planning for IT in SCM*: IT planning must have long-term vision to match the goals and objectives of SCM in terms of flexibility and responsiveness.
- *Virtual enterprise and collaborative commerce*: Establishing a network of firms, to create a virtual organization. The advanced version of this concept is called CFPR (collaborative forecasting, planning, and replenishment).
- *Infrastructure*: Apart from the software and hardware, the training of personnel in the use of the technologies needs to be taken care of on a regular basis.
- *Creating and managing knowledge*: With vast reservoirs of information being generated, there is a tremendous opportunity to generate knowledge to be competitive in the marketplace.

What Is Information Technology (IT)?

IT is an umbrella term that encompasses all forms of technology used to create, store, exchange, and use information in its various forms (business data, voice conversations, still images, motion pictures, multimedia presentations, and other forms, including those not yet conceived). It's a convenient term for including both telephony and computer technology in the same word. It is the technology that is driving what has often been called "the information revolution."—whatis.com

The information revolution has been considered the next revolution after the "railroad revolution or the transport revolution," that linked the whole country. IT has also impacted the management of supply chains. The question then arises, "what are the key issues in supply chain management that IT can help to address?"

Goals of Supply Chain Information Technology

The primary goal of IT in the supply chain was to link the point of production with the POS. However, this continues to change as we move toward more integration of IT in the supply chain. Specifically, as we digitalize the supply chain, we are able to connect the point of origin, point of production, POS, point of consumption, and the reverse supply chain. This not only allows planning, tracking, and estimating lead times based on real data, but also adds the ability for consumers to know the origin of their products and their components, for businesses to understand the reverse supply chain, for organizations and governments to trace product issues and substantially improves the transparency of the entire supply chain. To utilize information, we need to collect it, access it, analyze, and have the ability to share it for collaboration purposes. In this sense, supply chain system goals are as follows:

Collecting information: Everybody in the supply chain needs to know the status of their information. For this reason, it is important to be able to access the data that reside in locations inside a company. Moreover, the participants need to see data in different terms, therefore translation tables are required.

Access to data: The goal here is that all the available information can be accessed, regardless of the mode of inquiry used (e.g., phone, cloud, virtual access, etc.,) or who is making the inquiry. Ideally, everyone who needs to use certain data should have access to the same real-time data through any interface device, see Figure 7.1 (e.g., banking applications you can access the same account from almost everywhere).

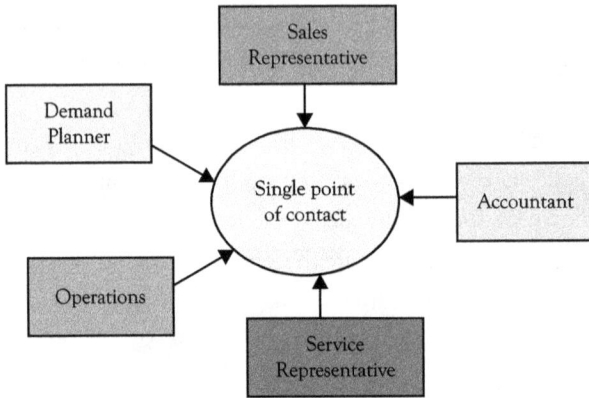

New generation of Information system

Figure 7.1 New generation of information system

Analysis based on supply chain data: The information must be analyzed and utilized to find the most efficient ways to produce, assemble, warehouse, and distribute products. To facilitate this, an IT system must be flexible enough to accommodate changes in supply chain strategies.

Collaboration with supply chain partners: The company's success depends on the ability to collaborate with partners. This requires not only sophisticated alignment of IT systems but also the integration of business processes. Collaboration has produced two systems: supplier relationship management (SRM) the ability to link and work effectively with suppliers and CRM to provide better contact and understanding customer needs.

IT Solutions for SCM

IT is primarily used for managing the flow of information across an organizations' supply chain. IT is also employed for efficient storage and retrieval of the information. Different technologies are used with different portions of the supply chain. Thus, we need to view various technologies from the perspective of where they fit in the supply chain.

The Upstream Supply Chain

Based on your role in the supply chain, the upstream part may consist of suppliers, manufacturers, or distributors. All the entities in the supply chain from which you are procuring the goods or services form the upstream part of the supply chain. Some of the technologies that are widely used with this portion of supply chain are as follows:

- **EDI:** EDI is commonly defined as computer-to-computer electronic exchange of business documents in a standard format. Benefits of using EDI:
  ○ Reduced costs for order processing.
  ○ Improved communication.
  ○ Electronic verification, automation, and less error-prone.
- E-Business: E-business is business primarily conducted over various networks using web technology to streamline business processes. Benefits of e-business:
  ○ Increased productivity and efficiency.
  ○ Trusted and easy communication with vendors, partners, and customers.
  ○ Redefine traditional business models to maximize customer experience. E-commerce is a facet of e-business.
- **Extranets:** Extranets connect several intranets via the Internet by adding to the Internet security mechanism. They form some kind of virtual network between organizations. The benefits of extranets in SCM:
  ○ Reduction of cooperation and operational costs.
  ○ Expedite and secure information delivery.

The Internal Supply Chain

The internal part of the supply chain includes all the in-house processes used in transforming the inputs received. The internal supply chain is mainly concerned with production management, manufacturing, and inventory control. The ways IT is used with internal supply chain:

- **Intranets:** An intranet is the use of the Web to create a private network of the organization. Some benefits of intranets are:
  ○ Increased availability of company information to trusted users.
  ○ Increased security by using firewalls or other safety mechanisms.

- **Data warehouses:** Proper storage and management of data is very critical. Data warehouses provide storage of data in different formats that are widely used. The advantage of using data warehouses is you can get all the information you want from one place. Access to the data in the warehouse is transparent to the user irrespective of its storage location.
- **ERP systems:** An ERP integrates all the applications related to the internal supply chain. Some benefits of using ERP software are:
  - Force business process reengineering. Business process reengineering (BPR) is an approach that aims at improving business tasks to achieve organization's goals.
  - Reduction of cost.
  - Multiple functionalities like data storage, transaction processing, planning, and so on may be provided as part of ERP software.
- **Transaction processing software:** The IT system in which the computer responds immediately to user requests. Also called Online Transactional Processing (OLTP). The benefits of using transaction processing software are:
  - Reduced overhead.
  - Faster response to customer demands and thus improves customer experience.
- **Executive information systems (EIS):** EIS is a set of forecasting and planning tools to assist senior management. The benefits of using EIS are:
  - Improved strategic planning.
  - Executive decision-making support.
  - Expedite business decisions.

The Downstream Supply Chain

The downstream supply chain includes all the activities in delivering the final products to customers who may be other organizations. Some of the emerging technology trends that are used are as follows:

- **Web services:** The web services provide service to customers or other businesses. These are self-contained, self-describing

modules aimed at application integration. Advantages of using web services:
- ○ Increased availability.
- ○ Easy to extend.
- ○ Increased interoperability with other systems.
- **Order management software:** System that receives customer order information and inventory availability from the warehouse management system and then processes the orders. The benefits of using this technology are:
  - ○ Determines the inventory levels and trigger actions automatically.
  - ○ Groups the customer order according to priority and requirements.
  - ○ Establishes order delivery dates and notifies customers.
- **CRM software:** CRM systems are used to keep track of a company's most valuable assets—their customers. The following are some benefits of using CRM software:
  - ○ Creates properly managed information about customers.
  - ○ Analysis and mining tools for extracting customer information.
  - ○ Automate the process and reduces paper overhead.

Advantages and Difficulties of IT

Time Management

Using an IT system that can measure several aspects of how much time is being used for processes and other business functions can aid a company in analyzing where time is being wasted, any bottlenecks in a process, and can show where time is best being utilized. This will help with scheduling manpower, purchasing, and manipulation to make organizations more efficient or productive by shortening the amount of time it takes to complete a given amount of work. Organizations adopt a clock time vision to the extent that schedules are developed to make reliable predictions of the points in time at which specific actions. At the halfway point, their actions change to allow them to meet the deadline effectively pacing and synchronizing their activities.

Improved Customer Experience

Customer experience management (CEM), an IT tool, immediately generates reports and analysis. Managers use this information to proactively respond to customer service and satisfaction issues. From the voice of the customer and integrating it into the research and development cycle, companies reduce the risk of developing products not required by the marketplace. Using CEM as an IT tool demonstrates the power of collecting relevant customer information, developing and implementing winning strategies, and measuring their results.

Social—Cultural Issues and Resistance

Users are reluctant to invest time to learn a new tool if they already know ways to perform tasks using culturally proven and familiar technology. IT, particularly the computer, is not culturally neutral. It often reflects the nature of the country that developed or manufactured it. One of the most distinct problems of the developing countries in fostering IT is their cultural difference from western societies where individualism and rationalism are accepted as the higher values of life. Some jobs require retraining, others, many of them unskilled, would disappear or would be replaced, with a cheaper alternative to personnel. Thus, the question of introducing IT in countries where the unemployment rate is increasing each year becomes important.

Expatriation

In a global economy, gathering information and using IT tools in different countries can be difficult. It is best to go into a country knowing the culture so that the right information can be gathered, and proper factors taken into account during analysis. Expatriation issues are a growing problem for many international firms. From an SCM perspective, the organization determines the importance of international operations and the nature of international assignment. It then develops activities that are necessary to prepare personnel for foreign assignments.

Important Developments for a Successful IT-Enabled SCM

Currently, companies are improving their organization in order to compete in an emerging world. Companies are now trying to improve their ability to be flexible and responsive in an electronically connected and dynamic world to meet the changing market. Companies need to intensify their efforts in developing information and communication technologies to overcome the complexity of the buyer–supplier system driving relationship. This can be done by changing traditional and fundamental product distribution channels and customer service procedures and training staff to achieve an IT-enabled supply chain. In this sense, some critical areas for the successful development of an IT-enabled SCM are as follows.

Strategic Planning for IT in SCM

Almost all companies are now focusing on strategic planning with the objective of developing long-term plans and making changes to their organizations in order to improve their competitiveness. Strategic planning of IT should support the long-term objectives and goals of SCM both in terms of flexibility and responsiveness to changing market requirements.

For example, IT will facilitate rapid partnership formation by making available the right information and developing a virtual enterprise. Some important issues to be considered in strategic planning are:

- **Marketing IT in SCM:** Companies need to reconfigure their resources to compete in a new market and meet the changing requirements. This requires organizations to have an effective supply chain or a physically distributed enterprise.
- **Economic reasons:** Factors such as customer requirements, competitors, and price force organizations to change the way they manage their operations. Unsurprisingly, flexibility and responsiveness are associated with cost.
- **Organizational reasons:** Strategic planning of IT in SCM includes organizational issues such as structure, awareness of management, business processes, strategic alliances, and

IT. All are factors that influence the overall performance of IT-enabled SCM.

- **Technological reasons:** Strategic planning involves decisions that affect the long-term performance of an organization. For example, lack of IT in an organization can make it obsolete and make it unable to not qualify as a partner in a virtual enterprise.

Virtual Enterprise in SCM

Virtual enterprise or virtual organization is based on developing a network of collaborative firms with necessary core competencies for reaching the market on time with the right product. To develop a network, companies require a communication system to accomplish supportive work. This could be achieved by utilizing various telecommunication technologies. Some important issues to be considered in virtual enterprise are:

- **Partnership:** It is necessary that a partnership be open to innovation and trust due to growing networks and services delivered through the Internet.
- **Virtual teams and supply chain:** Virtual teaming is the most appropriate mechanism to examine the relationship between all parties along the value chain.
- **Virtual enterprise and IT:** Virtual enterprise is based on similar strategies. Distance across the partners, however, may create communication problems later on.

E-Commerce

E-commerce can take a variety of forms such as EDI, Internet, intranet, extranet, commercial apps, e-mail, and others. The necessity of communication and coordination is required to support the inter-organizational sharing of resources and competencies. Some important issues to be considered in e-commerce are:

- **Purchasing:** Purchasing practice has multiplied tremendously since the increased popularity of e-commerce. Examples of this benefit are cost savings resulting from reduced paper transactions, shorter order cycle time, inventory reduction, and enhanced opportunities for supplier/buyer partnership through communication networks.

- **Operations:** The adoption of more integrated I-commerce models should strengthen the relationship between a network orientation and a global supply chain management. The Internet makes foreign markets more accessible and makes it easier to integrate overseas customers, suppliers, and intermediates into a closely managed supply chain relationship.

- **Collaboration:** Collaborating with suppliers can enable e-commerce to be more flexible. For example, Amazon.com and Walmart.com do not warehouse all of the items that are available to purchase through their e-commerce sites; instead, they partner with suppliers and merely facilitate the order and payment from the purchaser, and the supplier does the rest to ensure warehousing and delivery to the ultimate consumer.

Infrastructure for IT in SCM

Infrastructure for IT in SCM consists of Internet connectivity, hardware, and software including application system integration. Training and education for IT is important to understand so that the full technology can be utilized. There are different IT platforms and systems available to enable the application of IT in SCM. Some important issues to be considered in the infrastructure are:

- **Organizational:** Adaptation of e-business involves deep-level changes that affect core elements of an organization, including mission, vision, business strategy, goals, culture, technology, training, and policies. Organizational issues in infrastructure were caused by the Covid-19 pandemic, where companies around the world were having to divert to primarily virtual work (Newman and Ford 2021). This caused high percentages of companies, who were not originally used to being in an online setting, to adapt to the unfolding events and maintain productivity through the use of IT (Newman and Ford 2021).

- **Technological:** Technological innovations, such as advances in ERP systems, have come in abundance in the past decade that have played a major role in developing SCM. Also, developments in hardware and telecommunications technologies have occurred in order to meet the rising demand from companies. An increase in the amount of cyber security threats due to the Covid-19 pandemic has caused more companies to better develop their technological infrastructure to better combat these hackers (Pranggano and Arabo 2020).

Knowledge and IT Management in SCM

Knowledge management is concerned with recognizing and managing all organization's assets to meet its business objectives. Organizations have redesigned their internal and external structure, creating a knowledge network to facilitate improved communication data, while improving coordination, decision making, and planning. Some important issues to be considered in knowledge and IT management are:

- **Technology management:** Information technology such as XML for representing corporate data, ERP infrastructure that provide support for logistics operations, and web infrastructure allow B2B e-commerce success or SCM. In the emerging e-procurement marketplaces, firms establish efficient web-based electronic relationships that allow for closer integration between buyers and suppliers.
- **Educating and training:** Educating and training are the most important component of any change process in an organization. In order to be successful, companies need to have full cooperation of employees at all **levels**; otherwise, technologies alone will not help to improve the organizational competitiveness.

Implementation of IT in SCM

People and processes in an organization must adapt and learn in the processes of change to respond to the introduction of IT. The changes are often drastic and cause organizational tension. Integration of this supply chain's activities and processes before development and implementation of the information system in SCM is needed.

- **Organizational:** Top management support is a fundamental requisite for a successful implementation of IT. Also, the nature of skill available within an organization influences IT success as well.
- **Methodological:** Methodological issues of IT implementation in SCM are important too, some companies choose to reengineer their business process with the objective of implementing IT and improving their performance.
- **Cultural (Human Resources):** Such as the behavioral attitude toward the implementation of IT in SCM, level of education, knowledge in computers, international exposure, training and education, reward and employee empowerment, and incentive scheme impact the successful implementation of IT in SCM (Figure 7.2).

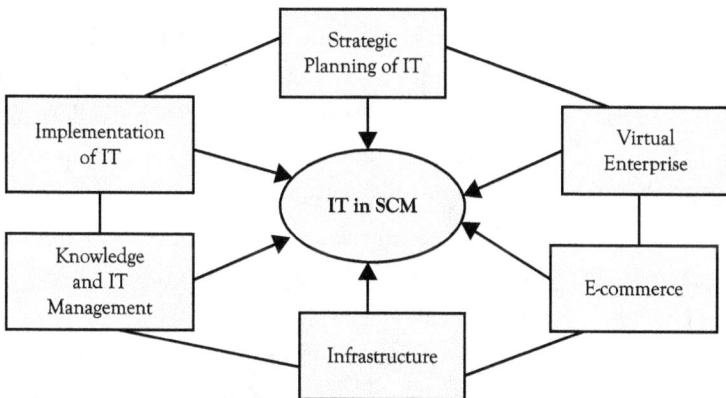

A framework for development of IT for effective SCM

Figure 7.2 IT impacts on SCM

An IT application is very important to a business' supply chain. The application needs to be able to gather needed data, store the data, and then retrieve the data so that it can be used in a meaningful and correct way. Some companies have been able to use and apply their IT systems so that they gain the upper hand in the competition.

Mini-Case: Dell and Walmart Stores

These two companies devastated their competition by reinventing their supply chains and are now firmly established as dominant players in their business.

Walmart uses a huge IT network to let suppliers know what and when products are needed. They are constantly in the forefront of new technologies trying to implement what they believe will support their strategic focus of low-cost operations.

Dell uses the Internet to manage ordering information. A customer puts in their order and the system assigns a barcode to the job. All the information on the product, from when it was built, how long it took at different processes to when it was shipped is stored in Dell's IT network and has helped with all types of forecasting.

Such IT applications use a mix of design and planning and may include modules for managing demand, distribution, production, material requirements, purchasing, and fulfillment. Some supply chain applications include multimodule systems for managing warehousing, transportation, customer relationships, and supplier relationships. There are also newer systems for monitoring the chain as a whole and responding to problems as they occur. These packages come from many vendors and are built using a wide range of technologies, which further complicates the integration process. Integration problems are gradually being solved, largely through major ERP vendors incorporating supply chain applications into their flagship products, but the industry hasn't yet matured to the point where installing supply chain software is reliable.

What happens when an IT system fails or is not used properly? The following are examples of the importance of keeping supply chains running smoothly. These companies lost major money, but these operational losses represent only part of the true cost of supply chain failures. The larger hit comes when companies reveal their mistakes to the financial markets.

Mini-Cases

Nike and Cisco Systems: These two companies ran into trouble with their supply chains. In the case of Nike, the company announced that sales for the preceding quarter were $100 million lower than expected because of confusion in its supply chain caused by a failed installation of i2 Technologies Inc.'s APS system. This loss was eclipsed by Cisco's announcement that it was writing down $2.2 billion in unusable inventory due to problems in its supply chain. The write-down was due, in large part, to a materials planning system that allowed demand for components to be double and triple counted across its suppliers.

Kmart Corp: The company announced in May 2000 that it was spending $1.4 billion on software and services to overhaul its supply chain, including planning systems and warehouse management software. A year and a half later, before the system went live, Kmart announced that it was abandoning most of the software it had purchased and was instead buying $600 million worth of warehouse management software from Atlanta-based Manhattan Associates Inc. This new push also failed to solve the company's supply chain problems, and it went into bankruptcy in January 2002.

Anderson Interfaith Ministries (AIM): AIM is a local faith-based organization that provides services such as a food pantry and other related assistance to underserved communities in Anderson, SC. During Covid-19 crisis in2020, the organization was struggling to find ways to keep the food pantry open to the public. In order to be able to provide these services no patrons could come inside the food pantry to retrieve items instead they had to be served outside. The management of AIM worked with students from a local university to develop an app so that patrons could check-in online and notify the organization that they were on their way to pick-up items and the items were delivered to their car. IT and ingenuity allow organizations to survive during crises while others that do not leverage all of their resources including IT tend to fail.

What can be learned from the failures? For starters, the industry needs to support yet another generation of enterprise applications, with all the growing pains and integration problems. Although SCM software forms a tidy category, it is an odd assortment of packages from a variety of vendors, which makes integration more complicated and information harder to obtain.

Key Takeaways

Integrating IT to one's company is a grand idea. It can add tremendous value to the company and make the supply chain more efficient. However, there are some concerns that need to be dealt with IT in SCM. Most of the IT used in the supply chain comes under the banner of "inter-organizational systems (IOS)" and there are many important factors that impact the success/failure of IOS.

- **Partners:** A collaboration that is willing to cooperate and work together is vital. There must be willing participants that are involved so that information sharing is possible even when the entities have different objectives and different partners.
- **Common technological standards:** IT is strictly dependent on technology, integration and data access. It is imperative that all companies keep up with industry standards so that all the information that is gathered can be accessed and used to help the supply chain run efficiently. This includes keeping up with emerging technology and taking the risk to change one's core business processes.
- **Education and training:** New technologies that are available must be taught to those people who will use the technology, so that the program is not underutilized.
- Cross-cultural **issues:** With the global economy, it is important to understand cultural differences so that it can be taken into account when data is analyzed.

- **Resistance to change:** With many new emerging technologies, a company must be willing to adapt and change strategies when it is necessary.

Variations of IT support for supply chain functions include:

- **Upstream Supply Chain:** EDI, E-business, extranet, and Internet with client/server scheme.
- **Internal supply chain:** Intranets, data warehouses, ERP, transaction processing software, and executive information systems.
- **Downstream supply chain:** Web services, order management software, and CRM software.

Reflection Points

1. How well do your IT systems support the goals of your supply chain? Do they support the integration and coordination of internal and external participants in your value chain? Which of the IT strategies listed above are not utilized by your company? Why?
2. Are you prepared for the digitization of the supply chain? Will your suppliers be ready to meet your requests and needs in this arena? How are you going to interact differently with suppliers and customers when there is full transparency in the supply chain?

Additional Resources

Bal, T. and P.K. Teo. 2000. *"Implementing Virtual Teamworking.* Part 1: A Literature Review of Best Practice." *Logistics Information Management* 13, no. 6, pp. 346–352.

Corsten, D. and T. Gruen. 2004. Stock-Outs *cause walkouts.*

Chopra, S. and P. Meindl. 2004. *Supply Chain Management: Strategy, Planning and Operation*, 2nd ed. New Jersey, NJ: Pearson.

Fisher, M. and A. Sheen. 2000. *Are You Ready?*

Grossman, M. 2004. *"The Role of Trust and Collaboration in the* Internet-Enabled *Supply Chain." Journal of American Academy of Business* 51, pp. 391–396. Cambridge: American Academy of Business.

Gunasekaran, A. 2003. *Information Systems in Supply Chain Integration and Management.* Elsevier.

Hewitt, F. 2001. *"After Supply Chains, Think Demand Pipelines." Supply Chain Management Review.* www.scmr.com.

Krishnan, R. 2001. *Technology in the Indian retail Supply Chain* 44, no. 6.

Kumar, K. 2001. *"Technology for Supporting Supply Chain Management." . Communications of the ACM* 44, no. 6, pp. 58–61.

Lee, H. 2002. *"Aligning Supply Chain Strategies With Product Uncertainties." California Management Review* 44, no. 3, pp. 105–119.

Lee, H. October 2010. "Don't Tweak Your Supply Chain—Rethink It End to End." *Harvard Business Review,* no. 10, pp. 62–69.

Lei D. and J. Slocum. 1992. *"Global Strategy,* Competence-Building *and Strategic Alliances." California Management Review.*

Newman, S. and R. Ford. 2021. "Five Steps to Leading Your Team in the Virtual COVID-19 Workplace." *Organizational Dynamics* 50, no. 1. https://doi.org/10.1016/j.orgdyn.2020.100802.

Pranggono, B. and A. Arabo. 2020. "COVID-19 Pandemic Cybersecurity Issues." Internet *Technology Letters* 4, no. 2. https://doi.org/10.1002/itl2.247.

Riska, J. 2002. *Customer Experience Management.*

Rutner, S. 2001. *Is Technology Filling the Information.* www. Scmr.com.

Ryssel, R., T. Ritter, and H.G. Gemünden. 2004. *The Impact of* Information Technology *Deployment on Trust, Commitment and Value Creation in Business Relationships* 19.

Saunders, C. and D. Vogel. 2004. *My Time or Yours? Managing Time Visions in Global Virtual Teams* 18, no. 1.

Seidmann, A. and A. Sundararajan. n.d. *Building and Sustaining Interoganizational Information Sharing Relationships: The Competitive Impact of Interfacing Supply Chain Operation With Marketing Strategy.*

Senn, J. n.d. *The Evolution of Interorganization Systems: Identifying the Stage.*

Simchi, D. and P. Kaminsky. 2003. *Designing and Managing the Supply Chain Concepts, Strategies and Case Studies,* 2nd ed. Boston, MA: McGraw-Hill/Irwin.

Turban, E. and J. Wetherbe. 2004. Information Technology *for Management,* 4th ed. New York, NY: John Wiley & Sons.

Varner, I. and T. Palmer. 2002. *"Successful Expatriation and Organizational Strategies." Review of Business* 23, no. 2, pp. 8–11.

Website Reference

www.inventorysource.com/ecommerce-website/ecommerce-terminology/.

Multiple Choice Questions

1. _____ is an umbrella term that encompasses all forms of technology used to create, store, exchange, and use information in its various forms.

   a. Virtual enterprise
   b. E-business
   c. E-commerce
   d. Information Technology
   e. Infrastructure

2. Which of the following technologies is used in an internal supply chain?

   a. EDI
   b. Data warehouses
   c. Customer relationship management
   d. Virtual private networks
   e. Order management systems

3. Which of the following technologies is used in an upstream supply chain?

   a. Customer relationship management
   b. Data warehouses
   c. Supplier relationship management
   d. Intranets
   e. Enterprise resource planning

4. Which of the following is an advantage of information technology?

   a. Users are reluctant to invest time into learning a new tool.
   b. Unskilled jobs would disappear or replaced with a cheaper alternative to personnel.
   c. Improved customer experience.
   d. Expatriation.
   e. It often reflects the nature of the country in which it was developed or manufactured.

5. Which of the following best describes a shared, immutable ledger for recording transactions, tracking assets, and building trust?

   a. Extranets
   b. E-business
   c. Transaction processing software
   d. Executive information systems
   e. Blockchain

6. What is not an important issue, as mentioned in the textbook, when considering strategic planning for IT?

   a. Economic reasons
   b. Political reasons
   c. Market IT in SCM
   d. Technological reasons
   e. Organizational reasons

7. _____ is essential for a successful implementation of IT.

   a. E-commerce
   b. Time management
   c. Customer service
   d. Top management support
   e. Decentralized infrastructure

8. What is not one of the changes to the work environment that occurred after the worldwide pandemic, Covid-19?

   a. Companies have purchased more IT hardware for home offices
   b. Videoconferencing has become more prevalent
   c. Employees are taking more vacations
   d. Employees have less commute when working from home
   e. Many companies have realized employees do not need to be in the office to work effectively

9. Which two companies were successful when they properly implemented changes to their IT?

    a. Walmart and Dell
    b. Nike and Cisco
    c. Cisco and Kmart
    d. Kmart and Nike
    e. Walmart and Nike

10. _____ is/are the most important component(s) of any
change in an organization?

    a. Leadership
    b. Education and training
    c. Technology
    d. Operations
    e. Human Resources

11. Which is not an important development that needs to be focused on
for successful IT enabled SCM?

    a. Information revolution
    b. Infrastructure
    c. Strategic planning for IT in SCM
    d. Virtual enterprise and collaborative commerce
    e. Creating and managing knowledge

12. Which of the following is not a goal of Supply Chain Information
Technology?

    a. Collecting information
    b. Access to data
    c. Analysis based on supply chain data
    d. The removing of bottlenecks
    e. Collaboration with supply chain partners

13. What uses the Web to create a private network of the organization?

    a. ERP systems
    b. Data warehousing
    c. Intranets
    d. Extranets
    e. EDI

14. Which of the following is an important issue to be considered in virtual enterprise?

    a. Purchasing
    b. E-commerce
    c. Educating and training
    d. Partnership
    e. Expatriation

15. Which company failed in properly implementing changes to their IT, causing them to go bankrupt?

    a. Dell
    b. Walmart
    c. Cisco
    d. Kmart
    e. Nike

CHAPTER 8

Strategy and the Supply Chain

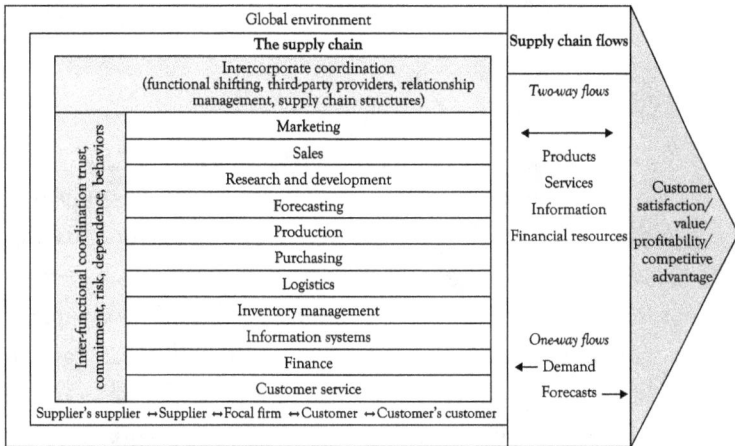

Chapter Objectives

- Continue discussion of strategic trading relationships
- Introduce key SCM strategy concepts
- Acknowledge uncertainty and variability in strategy

The goal of this section is not to reiterate the basis of SCM strategy. Instead, this chapter will highlight key strategy concepts and how they tie into SCM decisions. We will focus on how a company chooses to compete (its competitive strategy) and how that drives functional and operational strategy decisions that must be made by the various departments. In short, competitive strategy is one of the biggest factors in SCM decisions. Ultimately, there are only two competitive strategies:

- Cost
- Differentiation

The differentiation strategy can be broken into subgroups such as:

- Quality
  - High-performance design
  - Consistent quality
- Time
  - Fast delivery
  - On-time delivery
  - Product development speed
- Flexibility
  - Customization of products
  - Volume production flexibility

The key thing to notice is how a company's choice of competitive strategy drives other decisions. If you decide to compete on cost, then your supply chain must be geared to drive down costs at each opportunity. This is the competitive position of Walmart, which chooses suppliers that can provide low-cost mass-produced products and utilizes low-cost sea, truck, and rail logistics.

On the other hand, if you decide to compete by differentiation, there are other decisions to be made. Will you be competing on speed? Design quality? Conformance quality? Brand image? Each of these differentiation strategies (and there are more) require a different type of supply chain. To visualize this, compare the supply chain structure of Walmart (competitive strategy: low cost) versus that of FEDEX (competitive strategy: speed). FEDEX will make far more use of air-transport (fast but costly) than Walmart and its use of sea, truck, and rail transport.

Mini-Case: McDonald's in Russia

During the 1980s, McDonald's decided to open a facility in Moscow. McDonald's competitive strategy is low cost and conformance quality. In other words, McDonald's hamburgers taste the same anywhere you go in the World. In order to meet this goal of conformance quality and low cost, McDonald's was faced with several supply chain problems. Russia's road and rail network is extremely limited. Winston Churchill stated in the 1950s that there were no roads in Russia, only spaces between buildings. There was truth to that statement still in the 1980s. Thus, if McDonald's wanted to ship products into Moscow they would be forced to use airfreight which did not support their low-cost strategy. In addition, they could not purchase the foodstuffs locally, because the wheat, beef, cheese, and tomatoes (among others) did not meet their guidelines. Their final solution was to spend nearly 10 years building their own local supply chain. They went outside Moscow and built a ranch and farm, where they raised their own beef (so that the meat would taste the same), their own wheat (so the buns would taste the same) and their own vegetables. In this fashion, their supply chain matched their competitive strategy.

Managing a Supply Chain Strategy

As shown in Figure 8.1, developing a supply chain strategy requires the ability to plan for all factors that will affect you, your suppliers, and your customers.

Strategy is the unique position a company seeks to occupy in its industry. The supply chain must be designed to adapt to business activities and changing circumstances, as well as the goals that the business wants to achieve. Strategy change for any business, product, or supply chain can come in the form of revolution (radical change) or evolution (continuous improvement).

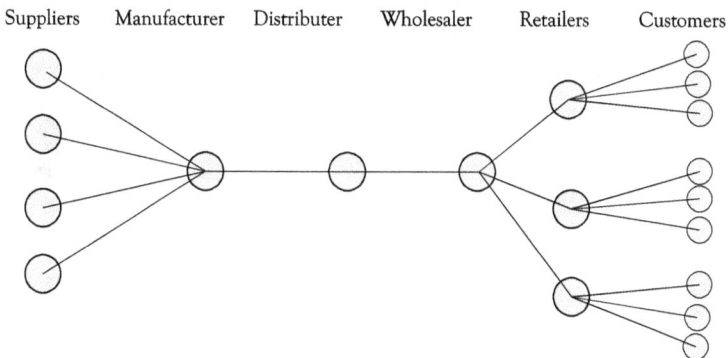

Figure 8.1 Traditional supply chain

The three key elements of managing a supply chain strategy:

1. Focus on the customer.
2. Match product type with the supply chain.
3. Include uncertainty and variability.

Focus on the Customer

What does your customer want? Customer service starts and ends with the customer because the loss of customer goodwill equates to lost sales. Remember that what a customer says they want and what they actually want can be two different things. Good supply chain managers must also be careful to not let their mental models cloud the analysis of what a customer wants. Every person's previous experience, training, and beliefs impact the data they see. This can lead to distortion. As a simplistic example, if I were to ask you what the basic reason people buy a car is, you might answer that it is transportation. What are the different motivations for people who purchase a Honda Civic, a Chrysler Minivan, a Ford F150 truck, and a Mercedes 560 SL? Applying this same concept to the supply chain may mean that instead of having three deliveries a week from you (a basic concept of JIT), a customer would prefer one a week but with 100 percent accuracy and a 10 percent discount. The following is a series of questions that supply managers should ask concerning their customers.

Know and understand your customer:

- Existing customers, that is,
  - Demographics
  - Existing and potential number
  - Income levels
- Who are your potential customers?
- How might your current and potential customers be grouped or segmented?
- What percentage of sales is contributed by each group?
- What are the preferred methods of communication for each of your customers (i.e., telephone, fax, e-mail, Internet telephony systems)?

- What do your customers expect from you?
- How well do your competitors meet customers' needs?

Match Product Type With the Supply Chain

Know thyself. The supply chain manager should understand the products, their production process, and how well they fit together strategically. Concerning the production process, one should know the following:

- Process flow
  - ○ Linear flow
  - ○ Job shop—batch flow
  - ○ Assembly line
  - ○ Continuous flow
  - ○ Project flow
- Order fulfillment strategy
  - ○ Make-to-order (e.g., Subway)
  - ○ Make-to-stock (e.g., McDonald's)

Once those questions are answered, they must be incorporated with another set of questions.

- What type of product are you producing?
- Are your products functional or are they innovative (e.g., socks versus fashionable clothes)?

Once you have established your product type you will know whether you need a physically efficient supply chain for a functional product or whether you will need a responsive supply chain for an innovative product.

Functional Versus Innovative Products

A supply chain strategy should consider the nature of the demand and the products. Products based on their demand fall into two main categories:

1. *Functional*—satisfy basic needs, do not change over time and have stable predictable demands with long life cycles. But they lead to lower profit margins (e.g., commodity items such as socks).

2. *Innovative*—offer higher profit margins but the demands are unpredictable, and their life cycles are short. For example, the basketball shoe market tends to fluctuate upon factors such as NBA players wearing certain shoes for a season.

Companies first need to determine whether their products are functional or innovative. Then decide whether their supply chain is physically efficient or responsive to the market because each of these products requires a different supply chain.

Supply chains perform two functions and incur costs specifically associated with each:

1. *Physical*—converts raw materials into finished goods.
2. *Market mediation*—tries to match the supply with the demand.

For functional products, market mediation is simple due to their nature as a commodity (i.e., socks) and physical cost needs to be minimized. For a company with functional products, the goal is physical efficiency that increases productivity and reduces costs all along the supply chain. Thus, functional products require an efficient supply chain.

The root cause of problems in many supply chains is the misalignment between the supply and the product strategies.

Many companies shift from functional to innovative products but leave their supply chains unchanged, thereby leading to a number of broken links in its supply chain. When a company has an unresponsive supply chain for innovative products, the right solution is to make some of the products functional and to create a responsive supply chain for the remaining products. It is important that manufacturers and retailers work together to cut costs throughout the system, especially in the case of functional products that are highly price sensitive. Uncertainty is inherent in innovative products and companies can either reduce, avoid, or hedge uncertainties in their system.

A technique that can be used as a tool in an innovative product and responsive supply chain atmosphere is mass customization. This is the concept of producing products to order but in lot sizes of one. Dell is one of the best examples of mass customization. While there are numerous ways to design a Dell computer, it is difficult to know what the customer will demand without listening to that customer. Dell began by configuring computers based on the specific demands of its customers rather than pushing products on them.

Uncertainty and Variability

There is not a single stage in the supply chain in which uncertainty and variability are not factors. The prudent supply chain manager must plan accordingly. Some ways to plan for uncertainty and variability is to collect statistical data on your suppliers, the manufacturing process and your customers, and use that information to create a system that is able to withstand the expected variations.

Forecasting is an unavoidable source of uncertainty and variability. Yet it must be done in order to estimate customer demand to fulfill customer expectations. Forecast uncertainty can come from three places within the supply chain:

1. Suppliers
2. Manufacturing processes
3. Customer demand

The uncertainty in customer demand can be measured through metrics such as average demand and the variability of the demand.

To decrease the uncertainty in the cycle, we can:

1. Use advanced analytical techniques to forecast demand.
2. Adopt reliable transportation modes.
3. Encourage suppliers to perform reliably.
4. Stabilize manufacturing processes.

Supply chain analysis is possible with reliable data and the right quantitative techniques. Analytical and statistical methods need data that involves a long collection process. Companies lacking current data show their carelessness toward uncertainty and ultimately toward affecting their strategies.

Key Takeaways

- Strategy comes in two versions: cost or differentiation.
- Differentiation can be created through quality, flexibility, and/ or speed.
- The three key elements of managing a supply chain strategy:
  1. Focus on the customer
  2. Match product type with the supply chain
  3. Include uncertainty and variability

Reflection Points

1. What is the competitive strategy of your firm?
2. Does your firm's supply chain strategy support the firm's competitive strategy?
3. How do your firm's customers benefit from your supply chain strategy?
4. Does your firm have more than one supply chain and supply chain strategy? Do you think this is feasible?

Additional Resources

Bolton, R. and K. Lemon. May 1999. "A Dynamic Model of Customers' Usage of Services: Usage as an Antecedent and Consequence of Satisfaction." *Journal of Marketing Research* 36, no. 2, pp. 171–186.

Carr, A. S. Muthsamy, and C. Owens. 2012. "Strategic Repositioning of the Service Supply Chain." *Organization Development Journal 30, no.* 1, pp. 63–78.

Dobosz, A., and A. Dougal. May/June 2012. "Releasing Supply Chain Value." *Supply Chain Solutions* 42, no. 3, pp. 72–74.

Frei, F.X. November 2006. "Breaking the Trade-Off Between Efficiency and Service." *Harvard Business Review* 84, no. 11, pp. 92–101.

Lee, H.L. and C. Billington. September 1993. "Material Management in Decentralized Supply Chains." *Operations Research* 41, no. 5, pp. 835–847.

Muzumdar, M. and N. Balachandran. October 2001. "The Supply Chain Evolution: Roles, Responsibilities, and Implications for Management." *APICS the Performance Advantage.*

Narayanan, V.G. and A. Raman. November 2004. "Aligning Incentives in Supply Chains." *Harvard Business Review 82, no. 11*, pp. 94–102.

Multiple Choice Questions

1. Mentioned in the mini-case, what strategy did McDonalds take to keep low cost and product conformance when they decided to enter into Russia?

   a. They built infrastructure such as roads and railways to bring in their raw materials.
   b. They built their own farms and ranches prior to opening their first Russian restaurants.
   c. They had raw materials air freighted into Moscow.
   d. They purchased locally sourced materials that met their product standards.
   e. They abstained from the Russian market until they were able to bring in materials at a lower cost.

2. Which is not an example of a functional product?

   a. Socks
   b. Ziploc bags
   c. iPhone
   d. Toilet paper
   e. Household cleaner

3. _____ is an unavoidable source of uncertainty and variability?

   a. Forecasting
   b. Customer demand
   c. Portfolio effect
   d. Functional products
   e. Order fulfillment strategy

4. Which of the following is a company that practices the make-to-order strategy?

   a. Titleist
   b. McDonald's
   c. Nike
   d. Subway
   e. Coca-Cola

5. Which of the following company's practices make-to-stock principles?

   a. Dell
   b. Subway
   c. BMW
   d. McDonald's
   e. Jersey Mike's

6. Which of the following is one of the areas in which forecasting uncertainty can derive from?

   a. Domesticity
   b. Customer demand
   c. Quality
   d. Partnerships
   e. Market mediation

7. Which of the following is not a question you should consider when trying to better understand your customer?

   a. How should the customer help me?
   b. Who are your potential customers?
   c. What do your customers expect from you?
   d. How might your current and potential customers be grouped or segmented?
   e. How well do your competitors meet customer needs?

8. Which of the following is not an example of an innovative product?

   a. What Britney Spears wore in her last music video.
   b. NBA players shoes worn during last season.
   c. Socks.
   d. 2020 Range Rover Sport.
   e. Apple iPhones.

9. _____ tries to match the supply with the demand.

    a. Market mediation
    b. Forecasting
    c. Demographics
    d. Quality control
    e. Differentiation

10. This company has a competitive strategy of speed.

    a. FEDEX
    b. Walmart
    c. Dell
    d. Nike
    e. Oracle

CHAPTER 9

Supplier Selection

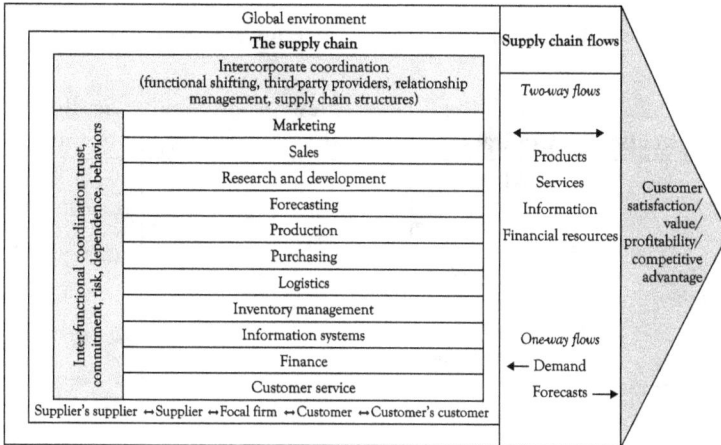

Global environment		
The supply chain	Supply chain flows	
Intercorporate coordination (functional shifting, third-party providers, relationship management, supply chain structures)	Two-way flows	
Marketing		
Sales	Products	
Research and development	Services	Customer satisfaction/ value/ profitability/ competitive advantage
Forecasting	Information	
Production	Financial resources	
Purchasing		
Logistics		
Inventory management		
Information systems	One-way flows	
Finance	Demand	
Customer service	Forecasts	
Supplier's supplier ↔ Supplier ↔ Focal firm ↔ Customer ↔ Customer's customer		

Interfunctional coordination trust, commitment, risk, dependence, behaviors

Chapter Objectives

- Introduce the concept of supplier selection
- Discuss the different types of supplier relationships
- Explore how internal purchasing organization affects supplier management

Supplier relationships are crucial to the organization. This is true whether they are transactional relationships based on single or few transactions between the parties or strategic relationships that may span decades in length with numerous transactions connecting the companies. These relationships should be managed intentionally and never treated as something that is taken for granted.

Strategic Alliances

Since SCM focuses on relationships, more firms are entering into strategic alliances such as those shown in the following table.

These can be categorized by level of commitment and strategic importance. See Figure 9.1.

Contractual Agreements		Equity Agreements		
Traditional Contracts	Nontraditional Contracts	No New Entity	Creation of New Entity	Dissolution of Entity
Arms-length Buy/sell contracts Franchising Licensing Cross-licensing	Joint R&D Joint product development Long-term sourcing Joint manufacturing Joint marketing Shared distribution Shared service Standard setting Research consortia	Minority equity investments Equity swaps	Joint ventures	Mergers Acquisitions
Licensing Cross-licensing	Joint marketing Shared distribution Shared service Standard setting Research consortia			

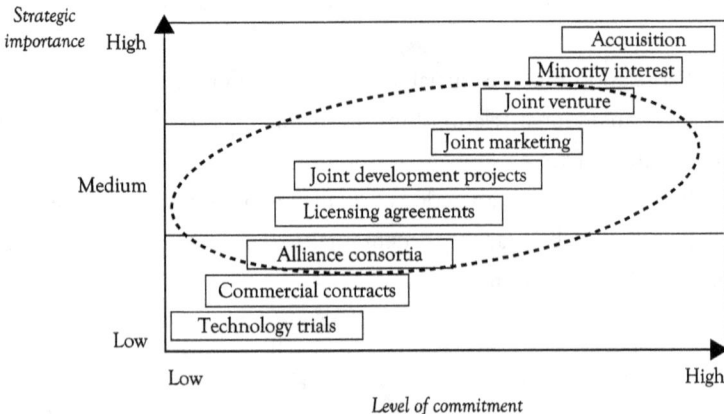

Figure 9.1 Level of commitment

Partnerships and Purchasing

Strategic alliances tend to be assessed and approached from a high-level, strategic perspective of a firm. On a more operational, day to day level, partnerships with suppliers are the most common and are usually managed through the purchasing department.

The key thing to remember is that instead of choosing suppliers purely based on low cost (which tends to mean that you have a large number of suppliers you chose from). You chose a few suppliers with whom you can build a long-term relationship. Thus, the criterion for choosing suppliers differs from the traditional approach. These are summarized as follows.

Traditional Approach	Supplier Partnerships
Primary emphasis on price	Multiple criteria
Short-term contracts	Long-term contracts
Evaluation by bids	Intensive and extensive evaluation
Many suppliers	Fewer selected suppliers
Improvement benefits shared based on relative power	Improvement benefits are shared are more equitably
Improvement at discrete time intervals	Continuous improvement
Problems are supplier's responsibility to correct	Problems are jointly solved
Clear delineation of business responsibility	Quasi-vertical integration
Information is proprietary	Information is shared

Outsourcing

Firms cannot be good at everything, which is why they sometimes turn to outsourcing. The decision to make (in-house) or buy (outsource) is a key managerial decision. It is portrayed in the following figure.

In practice, three of the four quadrants tend to be fairly easy to decide; however, the upper left-hand quadrant, Novelty Items, is the most difficult. It is this type of product that requires a "gut-check" decision to be made. Decision making in this quadrant also holds the greatest risk. See Figure 9.2.

High	**Novelty** (outsource/in-house) Technology quality	**Proprietary** (in-house) Technology quality service
Strategic value of the part in isolation	**Commodity** (outsource) Price	**Utility** (outsource) Cooperation
Low		service

Low   High

Criticality of the part to final assembly

Figure 9.2 Make vs. Buy Diagram

If a decision is made to outsource, the question then becomes who you will outsource this product or service to. Remember that the key issue in SCM is relationships. Specific criteria for this are as follows:

1. There is a MATURE, TRUSTING relationship with the BEST supplier in the category.
2. The supplier has a GOOD ENGINEERING capability.
3. The volume in the product category exceeds $1 million.
4. The product category involves a lot of TRANSACTIONS, creating a need for an in-plant representative.
5. The technology in the category is NOT changing at a revolutionary pace.
6. The category DOES NOT involve proprietary or core technologies (such as acoustics and electronics).

Decentralization Versus Centralization

When structuring your logistics and supply chain network, every structure is a variant of the extremes of centralized and decentralized. Both extremes have advantages, as shown in the following. The key is to focus on the needs of your particular firm and its strategic position. Your supply chain structure should follow from that.

Advantages of centralization include:

- Risk pooling/Variance reduction effect
- Economies of scale

- Economies of scope
- Learning/Experience curve
- Coordination advantages

Advantages of decentralization include:

- Product/Process improvements
  - ◦ Proximity to suppliers
- Customer satisfaction
  - ◦ Proximity to markets/customers
- Cost savings
  - ◦ Sourcing, production, logistics
  - ◦ Financing
- Risk diversification/Portfolio effect
  - ◦ Technology risk
  - ◦ Financial risk

A Short List of Practical Considerations

A good supply chain manager must remember that every situation is unique. While you can and should learn from what other companies are doing, each firm has its own unique set of characteristics that impact every managerial decision. This list is a compilation of practical considerations that each manager should keep in mind. They are general issues so that they can provide general guidance in a broad array of situations and companies.

- Logistics is the natural link between Operations and Marketing to make more efficient the flow of goods and information along the logistics system. Optimization of individual linkages does not guarantee global solutions and that is why you need a Global Logistics Approach for example, Resource Oriented Logistics, User Oriented Logistics, and Information Oriented Logistics.
- When determining and forecasting future demand, do not confuse historical sales with real demand. Try to incorporate substitution rates and information about stockouts. When measuring

service, don't confuse individual measures with order measures for example, mail orders versus POS information; link information with members of the logistics system via EDI, ECR (Electronic Collaborative Replenishment), CR (Collaborative Replenishment), and CFAR (Collaborative Forecasting and Replenishment); line fill rate versus order fill rate.

- Not all products (or customers) are equally important. Classify products according to logistics needs as well as financial indicators. SKU proliferation complicates logistics and SCM for example, ABC versus Organizational inventory (ORG), clear rules for introducing and retiring products from the market.

- Outsourcing is a great alternative for rationalizing the existing resources of a company; however, do not outsource without first analyzing the strategic fit with the core competence for example, strategic role of the part in isolation versus strategic role of the part to final assembly.

- 3PL companies are an excellent alternative for outsourcing logistics, however, make sure the needs as well as the specific measurement is determined in advance for example, show me the value measurement determination of the base case for comparison.

- What is your firm's competitive strategy? The strategy drives the requirements for a better understanding and management of the logistics and supply chain system. The best alliances are the ones where your strategic requirements mesh with those of your partner.

Key Takeaways

- Strategic alliances are necessary for global operations. They come in many different forms and types depending on the needs of your organization. SCM depends on relationship building and, as such, supply chain relationships should be considered strategically and not just be based on low costs or convenience.

- Outsourcing is a strategy that can provide competitive advantages to your organization if managed properly. Outsourcing decisions should be made with cross-functional teams and considered as part of the overall business strategy versus being reviewed in isolation.

Reflection Points

1. How have you utilized strategic alliances within your firm? Were you happy with the results? How well does your company manage strategic alliances that demand that multiple departments within your organization interact with your strategic partner? How are these types of complex relationships managed within your organization?

2. What outsourcing opportunities does your organization have available? Is the company taking advantage of these opportunities? Why or why not? What are your competitors outsourcing? Has your firm ever considered bringing functions back in-house that have been outsourced? Are there any functions now that should be considered for bringing back in-house?

Additional Resources

Christopher, M. 2000. Managing the Global Supply Chain in an Uncertain World. London, UK: Probity Research.

De Meyer, A., C.H. Loch, and M.T. Pich. Winter 2002. "Managing Project Uncertainty: From Variation to Chaos." *MIT Sloan Management Review,* pp. 60–67.

Dhillon, G. and J. Ward. 2002. "Chaos Theory as a Framework for Studying Information Systems." *Information Resources Management Journal* 15, no. 2, pp. 5–13.

Dobosz, A. and A. Dougal. May/June 2012. "Releasing Supply Chain Value." *Supply Chain Solutions* 42, no. 3, pp. 72–74.

Egelhoff, W.G. 1991. "Information-Processing Theory and the Multinational Enterprise." *Journal of International Business Studies* 22, no. 3, pp. 341–369.

Geary, S., P. Childerhouse, and D.R. Towill. July/August 2002. "Uncertainty and the Seamless Supply Chain." *Supply Chain Management Review* 6, no. 4, pp. 52–59.

Lee, H.L. 2002. "Aligning Supply Chain Strategies With Product Uncertainties." *California Management Review* 44, no. 3, pp. 105–119.

Lee, H.L. and C. Billington. September 1993. "Material Management in Decentralized Supply Chains." *Operations Research* 41, no. 5, pp. 835–847.

Lee, H.L., V. Padmanabhan, and S. Whang. 1997. "The Bullwhip Effect in Supply Chains." *Sloan Management Review* 38, no. 3, pp. 93–102.

Levy, D. Summer 1994. "Chaos Theory and Strategy: Theory, Application and Managerial Implications." *Strategic Management Journal* 15, pp. 167–178.

Muzumdar, M. and N. Balachandran. October 2001. "The Supply Chain Evolution: Roles, Responsibilities, and Implications for Management." *APICS the Performance Advantage*.

Omar, A., B. Davis-Sramek, M. Myers, and J. Mentzer. 2012. "A Global Analysis of Orientation, Coordination and Flexibility in Supply Chains." *Journal of Business Logistics* 33, no. 2, pp. 128–144.

Shore, B. 2001. "Information Sharing in Global Supply Chain Systems." *Journal of Global Information Technology Management* 4, no. 3, pp. 27–50.

Sterman, J.D. 1989. "Modeling Managerial Behavior: Misperceptions of Feedback in a Dynamic Decisions Making Experiment." *Management Science* 35, no. 3, pp. 321–339.

Sterman, J.D. 2001. "System Dynamics Modeling: Tools for Learning in a Complex World." *California Management Review* 43, no. 4, pp. 8–25.

van der Horst, J.G.A.J. and A.J.M. Beulens. 2002. "Identifying Sources of Uncertainty to Generate Supply Chain Redesign Strategies." *International Journal of Physical Distribution & Logistics Management* 32, no. 6, pp. 409–430.

Wilding, R.D. 1998. "Chaos Theory: Implications for Supply Chain Management." *The International Journal of Logistics Management* 9, no. 1, pp. 43–56.

Wilding, R.D. 1998. "The Supply Chain Complexity Triangle: Uncertainty Generation in the Supply Chain." *International Journal of Physical Distribution & Logistics Management* 28, no. 8, pp. 599–616.

Multiple Choice Questions

1. When determining and forecasting future demand, do not confuse _____ with _____.

   a. Risk pooling, risk diversification

   b. Historical sales, real demand

   c. Customer satisfaction, cost savings

   d. 3PLs, 4PLs

   e. Economies of scale, economies of scope

2. Which of the following is not an advantage of a decentralized supply chain?

   a. Cost savings
   b. Product/Process improvement
   c. Risk pooling
   d. Customer satisfaction
   e. Risk diversification/Portfolio effect

3. Which of the following is an advantage of a centralized supply chain?

   a. Economies of scale
   b. Proximity to suppliers
   c. Portfolio effect
   d. Logistics cost savings
   e. Proximity to markets

4. No matter the _____ of a firm, it is affected in some way by global competition or trading partners.

   a. Size
   b. Domesticity
   c. Location
   d. Strategy
   e. Flexibility

5. Which of the following is not a traditional approach to purchasing?

   a. Evaluation by bids
   b. Problems are supplier's responsibility
   c. Short-term contracts
   d. Fewer selected suppliers
   e. Primary emphasis on price

6. Established business relationships should be _____.

   a. Quid pro quo
   b. Arms-length
   c. Cherished
   d. Limited
   e. Fixed

7. Which of the following is not part of purchasing under the supplier partnerships approach?

   a. Equitable sharing
   b. Continuous improvement
   c. Problems are jointly solved
   d. Multiple criteria
   e. Clear delineation of business responsibility

8. Which of the following is not considered a product differentiator?

   a. Quality
   b. Time
   c. Flexibility
   d. Cost
   e. Brand image

9. _____ components should always be taken care of in-house.

   a. Commodity
   b. Utility
   c. Proprietary
   d. Novelty
   e. Noncritical

10. Novelty components can be taken care of in-house or outsourced. They have _____ strategic value and _____ criticality to final assembly.

   a. High; High
   b. Low; Medium
   c. Low; Low
   d. High; Low
   e. Low; High

11. No   matter   the   situation   supplier   selection   should   be
    _____.

    a. Intentional
    b. Commercial
    c. Strategic
    d. Applied

12. Advantages of centralization include:

    a. Risk pooling
    b. Customer satisfaction
    c. Proximity
    d. Risk diversification

13. Advantages of centralization include:

    a. Economies of scale
    b. Customer satisfaction
    c. Shared experiences
    d. Risk diversification

14. Advantages of centralization include:

    a. Economies of scope
    b. Longer learning curve
    c. Proximity
    d. Risk diversification

15. Advantages of decentralization include:

    a. Risk pooling
    b. Economies of scope
    c. Proximity
    d. Economies of scale

CHAPTER 10

Customer Service

Global environment		
The supply chain	Supply chain flows	
Intercorporate coordination (functional shifting, third-party providers, relationship management, supply chain structures)	Two-way flows	
Marketing		
Sales	Products	
Research and development	Services	Customer satisfaction/ value/ profitability/ competitive advantage
Forecasting	Information	
Production	Financial resources	
Purchasing		
Logistics		
Inventory management		
Information systems	One-way flows	
Finance	← Demand	
Customer service	Forecasts →	
Supplier's supplier ↔ Supplier ↔ Focal firm ↔ Customer ↔ Customer's customer		

Inter-functional coordination trust, commitment, risk, dependence, behaviors

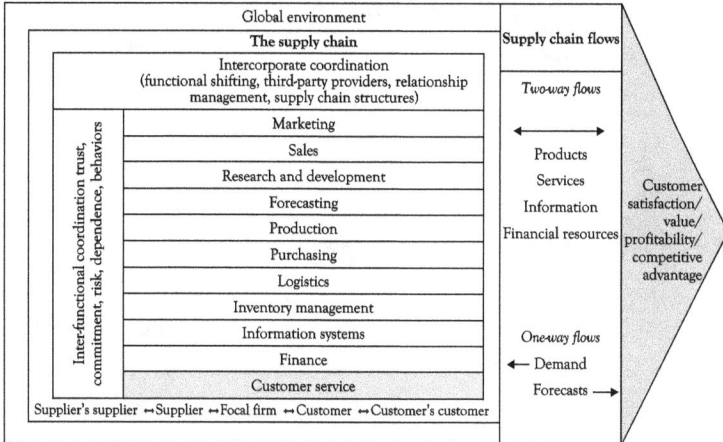

Chapter Objectives

- Introduce customer service as an SCM concept
- Discuss customer satisfaction
- Explore service quality
- Consider how to measure and manage performance
- Examine the balanced score card concept

William Davidow and Bro Uttal in their book, *Total Customer Service*, state that "the war of business has shifted onto a new battle ground ... The spoils will go to those few companies that both perceive the need for outstanding service and take the steps necessary to delivery it." Many companies have embraced the idea that they need to focus on customer service. What they have neglected are the actions necessary to actually deliver it.

In order to deliver exceptional customer service through the supply chain we need to view it in the context of a service supply chain. For example, Figure 10.1 outlines what supply chain managers should focus

Defining the strategic context
- Know your customers
- Develop service strategies
- Set objectives/standards
- Shape expectations
- Create a service culture

Recognizing and rewarding performance
- Reward high performers
- Share successes

Building the organization
- Design the service delivery system
- Provide organizational support
- Staff your service

Satisfying customer needs

Measuring and evaluating performance
- Monitor service behaviors/results
- Solicit customer and employee feedback
- Evaluate performance
- Keep score

Developing capabilities
- Develop managerial skills
- Enable frontline employees

Managing performance
- Lead by example
- Reinforce service values
- Manage the customer relationship

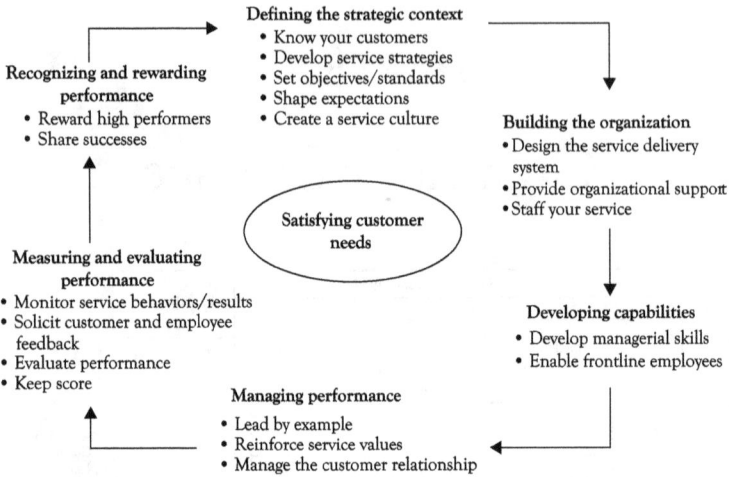

Figure 10.1 The service quality management process

upon in order to provide not only customer service but also customer satisfaction. The total service quality management process is the summation of focusing on the various elements of the cultural, social, and legal environment while aggressively managing your human resource and supply chain operations.

The strategic context is stooped in the cultural, social, and legal environment. With data on customer expectations within different environments and situations, a company will know what to do to keep customers satisfied, and will have the necessary information to set successful objectives and service standards.

Supply chain operations have a greater influence in the second step—building the organization. It is in this step that the service delivery system is designed, and a sound supply chain is the foundation of the delivery system. The importance of human resources can be seen in the majority of the service quality management process steps. Human resources are responsible for developing capabilities and managing performance, which includes measuring, evaluating, and recognizing performance, along with rewarding high performers. Hence, this conceptual framework can be used to manage high service quality in any industry. This chapter will outline some of the key concepts in this process.

Customer Service as a Supply Chain Concept

Today, many companies have a customer service standard, which is a statement of goals and acceptable performance for the quality of service that a company expects to deliver to its customers. This is all well and good, but what many companies fail to realize is that service operations (which encompasses all aspects of customer service) is a supply chain concept. Specifically, the customer experience is a chain of contacts the customer undergoes in obtaining a product as shown in Figure 10.2. Each link represents a contact. Just as in SCM, the total experience depends on the weakest link.

Thus, the customer experience includes any episode in which the customer comes in contact with the organization. This includes contacts via person, phone call, mailing, advertising, and Internet interactions, just to name a few. Thus, any event that forms a perception of the organization in the mind of the customer (both positively and negatively) can impact potential sales. That is why service operations are so important to SCM. Let's take a moment for a quick mini-case to emphasize this point.

Mini-Case Study: Caterpillar Corp.

Caterpillar is the world's leading manufacturer of construction and mining equipment, diesel and natural gas engines, and industrial turbines. One of Caterpillar's key SCM strengths is its ability to provide over 6,20,000 discrete service parts to keep customers up and running even when they are literally around the globe. Former Caterpillar Chairman Don Fites often referred to product support as the "corporate jewels." The reason for that is Caterpillar customers rate product support as the number one factor in generating repeat business.

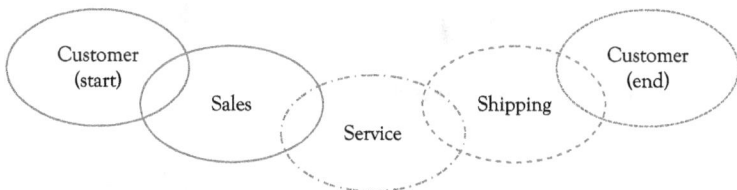

Figure 10.2 Customer service—a supply chain concept

This capability is not taken for granted; during the last 15 years, Caterpillar has continually improved its service parts supply chain. That improvement has been measured by reducing inventory by more than half while improving on customer service levels that were already the envy of the industry. Their customer service supply chain performance can be measured in various ways. For example, over 99 percent of the time, Caterpillar can ship an order in less than 24 hours. This would be impossible to accomplish without an efficient supply chain, and Caterpillar's supply chain productivity has increased by more than 60 percent during that time. All these metrics reflect particular operational issues, but all of them combine into savings. For Caterpillar, their improvements have saved the company more than $460 million annually—while continuing their outstanding customer service.

Customer Service by Understanding the Environment and Customer

Service operations consist of all company operations that are not purely manufacturing. Services can be broadly divided into two groups, those that are purely services and those that are associated with the manufacturing sector. In the purely service sector they can be further divided into public and private. Examples include:

- In the public sector:
  (a) Health
  (b) Social services
  (c) Local authority services (i.e., schools, recreation, parks).
- In the private sector:
  (a) Cleaning
  (b) Laundry
  (c) Hotels and restaurants
  (d) Banking
  (e) Insurance.

Service operations in the manufacturing sector are supporting functions such as transport and distribution, office services, maintenance, customer support, and so forth. As products across industries become commodities, superior service is often left as the last true differentiator between companies. Being customer-centric, therefore, is no longer a "nice-to-have" ideal, but a necessary ingredient for success.

Knowing the Customer and Customer Retention

In moving toward a more customer-centric service model, a company must know how to approach customer service. Building stronger and more profitable customer relationships is crucial in today's global market. This is a powerful competitive weapon that companies have available in order to retain customers; however, there is not a specific recipe for building such relationships. As customers differ from place to place, and business to business, the strategies needed to build strong customer relationships vary accordingly. For this reason, knowing who your customers are and what their expectations are (even when they are changing) becomes essential. There are 10 common expectations that management should keep in mind.

1. Be accessible;
2. Treat customers with courtesy;
3. Be responsive to customers' needs and wants;
4. Do what you are asked to;
5. Provide well-trained and informed employees;
6. Tell customers what they should expect from you;
7. Meet your commitments and keep your promises;
8. Do it right the first time;
9. Follow up;
10. Be socially responsible and ethical.

The fact that not all customers are the same holds an opportunity for companies rather than a constraint. When companies handle customers differently based on needs and expectations, the value of each customer relationship, which is based on customer segmentation, will be optimized. Companies not only need to understand customer needs, but they also need to anticipate those needs whenever possible. Only then companies will be able to make the right offer to the right person at the right time.

In order to deliver quality service to customers, companies need to continually enhance customer experiences in the competitive marketplace. Evidence indicates that satisfying customers, however, is not sufficient to retain them. In fact, what determines the loyalty or defection of a customer depends on how delighted or outraged a customer is with the company's behavior. Thus, focusing on customer delight and outrage may lead to a better understanding of the dynamics of customer emotions and their effect on consumer behavior and loyalty. On one hand, when customer needs are gratified with reliability, responsiveness, and assurance, they will be delighted. On the other hand, when customers' needs or desires are violated, they will be outraged.

The economics of attracting and retaining customers underscores the reason behind placing customers—not products—at the center of operations. Research consistently shows that it is five to seven times more expensive to find a new customer than to retain an existing one; however, it is prudent to remember that only valuable customers are worth retaining. All too often, in our experience, unprofitable customers are retained at detrimental expense to the company. Customer relationships must be aggressively managed, and those that are unprofitable, detrimental, or both, to the company should be severed. But, it does not mean that you should mistreat "low value" customers since you have an image and reputation to maintain in a specific industry. This simply means that the company should be keenly aware of its profitability by customer and understand the impacts of each customer's needs and desires on the company as a whole so that well-informed decisions can be made with regard to customer retention.

Customer Satisfaction

Generally speaking, high customer satisfaction can generate repurchase intentions, favorable word-of-mouth, and loyalty. There are three main components of customer satisfaction: price, product quality, and service quality. These are the components that a company can control. Situational and personal factors will also affect overall customer satisfaction, but these cannot be controlled, see Figure 10.3.

For a company to be customer- or demand-driven, it must know who needs what, and when they need it. This information must be available

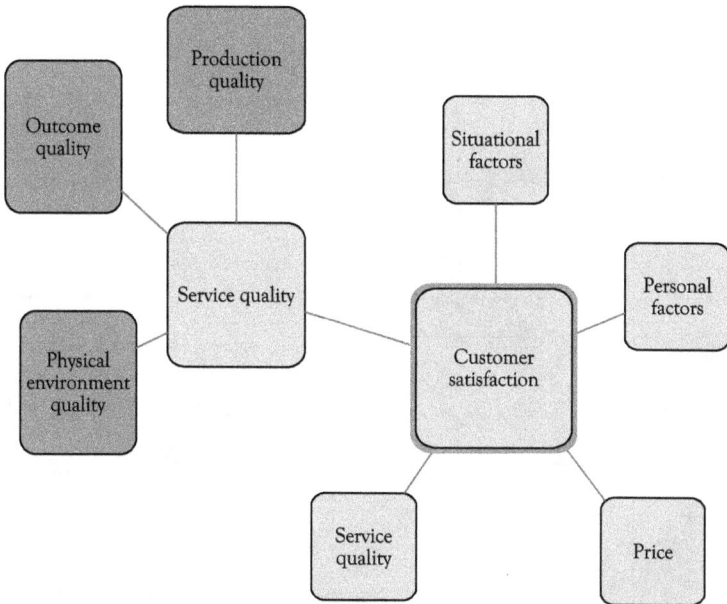

Figure 10.3 Factors impacting customer satisfaction

across the organization with as much lead time as possible, so that managers can create and assign the most efficient schedules and routes for delivery as possible. By obtaining a better understanding of demand, the company can improve the economics of each delivery while still ensuring customer satisfaction. All the previous elements determine how consumers perceive a company's service quality. In an attempt to establish a competitive advantage, marketing practitioners often seek to differentiate their offering upon service quality to ensure customer satisfaction.

A Gaps model of service quality was developed in the late 1980s. This model shows five gaps that can affect, either positively or negatively, service quality and customer satisfaction. If each element of this model is well understood, managers can easily recognize where they hold weaknesses and make the required modifications to increase customer satisfaction (Figure 10.4). The five gaps fall between:

- What customers expect and what managers perceive they expect (Gap 1);
- Managers' perceptions of customers' expectations and the actual specifications they establish for service delivery (Gap 2);

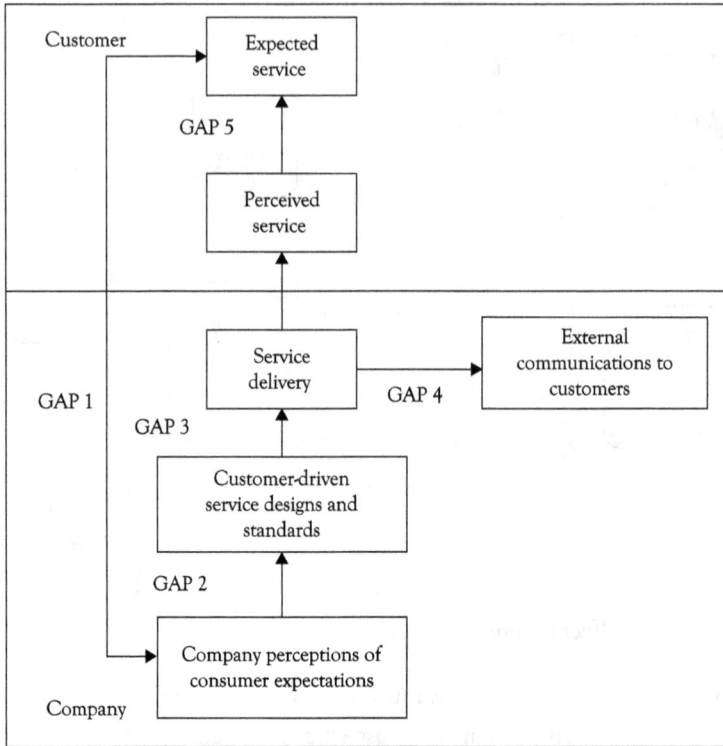

Figure 10.4 Gaps model of service quality

- Service specifications and the actual service delivered (Gap 3);
- What a company promises about a service and what it actually delivers (Gap 4); and
- Expected and perceived service from the customers' standpoint (Gap 5, the net effect of the last four gaps).

Service Quality: Building the Organization and Developing Capabilities

Service quality is an important precursor of customer assessment of values. It will in turn influence customer satisfaction and motivate behavioral intentions. In other words, the way a company manages its service operations reflects on how customers perceive the service quality. In order to establish competitive advantage, marketers often seek to differentiate their service offering upon service quality. There are both external and internal factors that will influence service quality. Social and legal environments, along with culture, are the external factors the company should understand and be prepared to react to accordingly. With respect to the internal factors, human resources, and the supply chain, the company has to manage them in such a way as to meet the maximum number of customers' needs and desires to ensure high-quality service.

Culture

Culture is an accumulation of learned meaning within a human population. These learned meanings or values provide guidance in their behavior as consumers. Recent research suggests that culture plays a fundamental role in determining how consumers perceive what constitutes service quality. Different cultures provide consumers with rules that guide their evaluation of service quality simply because what is feasible in a country might not be feasible in another country. Since it is challenging to integrate individuals of diverse backgrounds into a coherent organization, one has to be culture sensitive in order to deal with conflicts that emerge as a result of cultural differences. Transferring new procedures and concepts to members of another culture are more difficult than imagined. Also, learning to operate within a new culture involves questioning and articulating previously taken-for-granted beliefs and assumptions.

Knowledge of the local culture is important in order to recognize differences in consumer behavior. Even if the company is successful in managing cultural conflicts within the organization, it faces yet another challenge in order to understand local customers. They may have particular needs, expectations, and service quality perceptions with which the company has no experience. Redesigning operations may be necessary to meet and exceed those new expectations to ensure a high-quality service perception. That is why standardization is not always possible and a degree of flexibility is highly desirable. For instance, McDonald's had to completely forgo its "beef specialty" and instead offer lamb and veggie patties in India.

Social and Legal Environments

Global markets mean that there are many countries offering immense opportunities for international companies, but their success often hinges on how they adapt their operations to the diverse social and legal environments in different localities. Even though these factors are external to the company, they often have huge influence on many areas of the company's operations. As an illustration, McDonald's, an active proponent of diversity, offers separate dining sections for men and women in Saudi Arabia to suit the local social environment. Pizza Hut's Moscow facility presents one of the examples of issues to be addressed in a foreign legal environment. Owing to local laws, Pizza Hut had agreed to transfer management of the joint venture over to Russians eventually. Therefore, whether the Russian managers would be able to take over operations and maintain a high service quality became a major concern.

Human Resources Management

An organization that knows how to grow globally translates its winning people and employment practices into many different cultural settings. This cultural sensitivity spills over to the company's HR practices. Many successful companies employ positive and customer-service-oriented people while ensuring that all the employment practices, policies, and regulations are met. As the company moves through its selection process, it looks at specific skill, general knowledge, customer service abilities, and experience in potential employees. Since finding, developing, and retaining the best people is one of the most important functions in HR, it can be seen as an integral part of the success of a company. As it was stated in McDonald's 1994 annual report,

> In a copycat world, the best way to stand out from the crowd is through customer satisfaction—100% of the customers, 100% of the time ... It's no longer enough to measure restaurant performance by our internal standards, no matter how exacting. Success has to be measured through the eyes of the customer and the people who serve them.

Therefore, HR is a crucial factor to service operations. Its value can be seen as hiring, training, developing managerial skills, appraising, rewarding, and retaining the right managers and employees. The people who interact with customers should be carefully selected and trained to be able to deal with unexpected situations. Many times, it is not the problem that makes the customer dissatisfied but the inability of employees to promptly react to that situation. Proper training can prepare employees better for such situations, but it is also a matter of selecting people with the right attitude and giving them some degree of autonomy to make decisions themselves. As a motivation to maintain high performance levels, performance has to be constantly evaluated and high performers rewarded. Also, the role of the employees "behind the counter" should not be underestimated. Often, the last touch point of customer service is the only one that the customer evaluates for total service quality and overall customer satisfaction.

Managing and Measuring Performance

Supply chain operations support service at the counter by physically making the transaction or the experience at the counter possible. Some of the operations include but are not limited to:

- Information systems platform;
- Data management;
- Order management;
- Distribution;
- Inventory management;
- Network strategy;
- Performance management;
- Transportation; and
- Vendor management.

Many supply chain managers believe that customer satisfaction occurs at the counter. While the experience of the customers with the employees at the "counter" is very important, the whole range of operations behind the counter is important as well. Thus, SCM managers should understand that all the operations that start from raw materials till the product is handed over to the customer, or the service is rendered to the customer, are equally important. Supply chain operations make it possible for customers to have what they want, when they want it, and how they want it.

Pareto Analysis

In addition, SCM techniques can also be applied to service operations. For example, a classic operations management technique used in SCM is the Pareto principle, otherwise known as the 80–20 rule. It applies, in multiple situations, and suggests that 80 percent of the effects come from 20 percent of the causes. For example, as a general rule, 20 percent of machine problems will cause 80 percent of the system errors. Another example in service operations can be seen in that usually 80 percent of the turnover (i.e., inventory movement) can be ascribed to approximately 20 percent of the customers, articles, or orders.

Using such a tool a company can

- Rank the customers, products, and so on, in order of magnitude;
- Calculate the percentage that each item contributes to total value;
- Derive a cumulative percentage list; and
- Evaluate the cumulative list and identify appropriate breakpoints (A, B, and C categories).

Table 10.1 is presented as an example. It helps to identify the customer groups, their primary expectations, and their contribution to total sales.

Note that customer 4 only contributes 6.3 percent of total sales and their expectations are the most lenient (six weeks from order to delivery); thus placing them as a category C customer is easily acceptable. While it may seem anathema to rank customers, it is true that not all customers are equal. It may prove both strategically and operationally efficient to choose not to respond to some customer requests. For example, this type of decision would make strategic sense if the volumes of products that are

Table 10.1 Pareto customer analysis

Customer	Sales	% Total Sales	% Cumulative Sales	Products	What the Customer Wants
1	92,000	18.4	18.4	A	3 days ex stock
2	83,500	16.7	35.1	A (75%) B (25%)	2 weeks
3	73,200	14.6	49.7	B	5 days ex stock
4	31,500	6.3	56	C	6 weeks order to delivery
Total Sales	5,00,000				

shipped to a particular customer were some of the highest, while the sales value were some of the lowest. Thus, by eliminating this customer, the supply chain has capacity freed up to increase customer service to higher value customers. Of course, it can be argued that the better solution is to develop a supply chain that can supply all customers with high service levels; however, that is not always feasible.

Performance Criteria and Metrics

Other SCM methods can support service operations. Table 10.2 provides several examples of service quality criteria. These are important so that performance metrics can be assessed and monitored, so that each dimension of service quality can be aggressively pursued.

Once particular criteria have been determined, then specific SCM metrics can be assessed. For example, overall customer service level can be measured as the desired probability versus the actual percentage that product demand can be met from stock. This can be expressed in a number of ways:

- Percentage of orders completely satisfied from stock.
- Percentage of units demanded, which are met from stock.
- Percentage of units demanded, which are delivered on time.
- Percentage of time there is stock available.

Table 10.2 Examples of service quality criteria

Service Quality Dimension	Criteria
Reliability	• Billing accuracy • Order accuracy • On-time completion • Promises kept
Responsiveness	• On-time appointment • Timely call-back • Timely confirmation of order
Assurance	• Skills of employees • Training provided to employees • Honesty of employees • Reputation of firm
Empathy	• Customized service capabilities • Customer recognition • Degree of server–customer contact • Knowledge of the customer
Tangibles	• Appearance of the employees • Appearance of the facility • Appearance of customers • Equipment and tools used

Specifically, reliability performance metrics might include percentage of items shipped without errors, percentage of goods delivered on time, and percentage of goods shipped without damage.

Responsiveness might be measured through assessing speed (reduced order–cycle time), flexibility (time required to respond to custom requests), and malfunction recovery (response time to respond to service failures such as the wrong product being shipped).

Balanced Scorecard

One key aspect to remember is that the **entire** supply chain impacts a customer's experience. Thus, it is of even greater importance to view and measure the performance of the supply chain as a whole, rather than just individual components. One way of doing this is through a technique called the balanced scorecard. The balanced **scorecard** is an analytic framework for translating a company's vision and high-level business strategy into specific, quantifiable goals and for monitoring performance against those goals. The methodology breaks high-level strategies into objectives, measurements, targets, and initiatives. It does this by improving an organization's performance in the four general areas of financials, customer perspective, business, and learning processes. This type of analysis is easily tied into SCM. An example is shown in Figure 10.5.

Robert S. Kaplan and David Norton, who wrote an article about it in 1992 for the *Harvard Business Review,* are usually credited with the idea for the balanced scorecard. Today many companies use one or more of its principles without having formally adopted the **balanced scorecard** methodology. As Arthur Schneiderman, an independent business-process management consultant, states, "There are many different **balanced scorecards,** and they serve many different purposes. But most organizations will say its purpose is to link strategy to action."

A key element to a successful service supply chain is tying the customer's perspective to that of the organization; creating and utilizing balanced

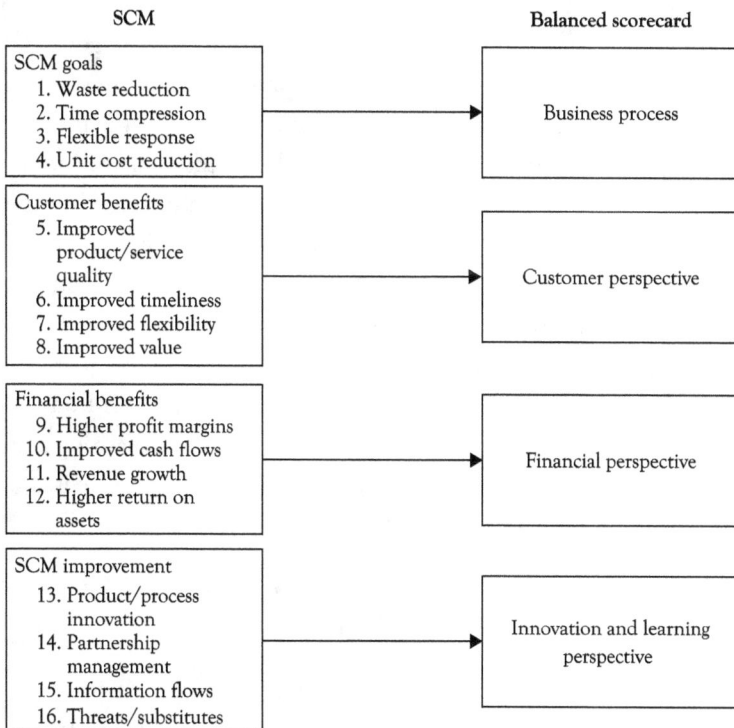

Figure 10.5 Comparing SCM measures to balanced scorecards

scorecards can give the organization a tool to do just that. By focusing on the elements discussed in this chapter—focusing on customers, improving personnel, and being culturally sensitive, companies can be ready to confront the cost and performance pressures in the global market that is focusing more and more on service operations as a differentiator. More importantly, they will have the strategic flexibility—the right tools, information, and organizational structure—to help position them for future growth while staying ahead of the pack.

Mini-Case: Southwest Airlines Co.

Southwest Airlines Co. employs a number of balanced **scorecards**, including one that relates ground crew performance to company profitability. Directly relating a financial measure such as "lower costs" with an operations metric like "fast ground turnaround" is a new idea at the Dallas-based airline, says Mike Van de Ven, Vice President of Financial Planning and Analysis. "Historically, the budget system was the primary system to monitor costs, and if you were an accountant, you got it," he says. "But if you were an operations person, and you weren't used to cost centers and general ledgers and budget-to-actual variances, it didn't make any sense to you." The operations people had hundreds of metrics dealing with things such as on-time performance or baggage delivery, but they weren't linked directly to the financial measures or the budget system, Van de Ven says. "So what we have been doing over the past several years is putting these things together, and that neatly rolls into this **balanced scorecard** concept." Another advantage of this integrated **scorecard** approach is that it retains the hundreds of detailed metrics for front-line supervisors but gives top management a "dashboard" summarizing a few key measures. Van de Ven states, "We are trying to get more focused on key measurements that we want to stay on top of."

Key Takeaways

- The ultimate goal of any supply chain is to satisfy your customers' needs in a way that is profitable to your company in the long run.

- The "customer experience" is a chain of contacts that the customer undergoes in obtaining a product or service. Managing the customer experience must be done from the customer's perspective throughout the supply chain.
- Service operations in the manufacturing sector are supporting processes such as transport and distribution, administration, maintenance, customer support, and so forth.
- Customer service requires anticipating customer expectations and continually enhancing their experiences.
- Transferring new procedures and concepts to members of another culture are more difficult than may be initially imagined. Also, learning to operate in a new culture involves questioning and articulating previously taken-for-granted beliefs and assumptions.

Reflection Points

1. Does your firm view service operations as a key aspect of SCM or is it viewed as a secondary issue? Do you know if your view of customer service is the same as your managers and employees?
2. One of the key difficulties in service operations can be summed up in this phrase "how do you train people to be nice?" How does your company approach training people to be nice? Do employees have to serve each other well before they can serve the customers well? Do your employees serve each other well?
3. In this chapter, it was mentioned that not all customers are equal and that a Pareto analysis can be useful in determining who your most important customers are and which customers might need to be dropped. Do you agree with this viewpoint or do you feel that the customer is always right? Are all customers worthy of keeping as customers? When is the last time you chose to keep an unprofitable customer?
4. What are some of the SCM metrics that your company captures that can be used to support service operations? What metrics in your company can easily be tied to financial results and communicated to employees?

5. What are some opportunities in your organization for balanced scorecards? Have you ever seen the scorecards that your customers keep on you? For example, Walmart scorecards their vendors. If you don't know if your customers keep a scorecard on your performance, ask them. And, if they do, ask if you can learn more about how they are measuring your performance so that you can work together as a team to improve your customer service. If you don't know what your customer wants, it is hard to satisfy them 100 percent of the time.

Additional Resources

Bolton, R. and K. Lemon. May 1999. "A Dynamic Model of Customers' Usage of Services: Usage as an Antecedent and Consequence of Satisfaction." *Journal of Marketing Research* 36, no. 2, pp. 171–186.

Carr, A., S. Muthsamy, and C. Owens. 2012. "Strategic Repositioning of the Service Supply Chain." *Organization Development Journal 30, no. 1,* pp. 63–78.

Donovan, J. 2003. "RF Identification Tags: Show Me the Money." *Electronic Engineering Times* 41.

Elllis, S. and S. Lambright. 2002. "Real Time Tech—Unilever Sees Intelligent Product Tags as the Brains Behind Real-Time Supply Chains." *Optimize* 44.

Frei, F.X. November 2006. "Breaking the Trade-Off Between Efficiency and Service." *Harvard Business Review* 84, no. 11, pp. 92–101.

Gilliland, M. and D. Prince. 2001. "New Approaches to 'Unforecastable' Demand." *Journal of Business Forecasting Methods & Systems* 20, no. 2, pp. 9–13.

Karkkainen, M. and J. Holmstrom. 2002. "Wireless Product Identification: Enabler for Handling Efficiency, Customisation and Information Sharing." *Supply Chain Management: An International Journal* 7, no. 4, pp. 242–252.

Lee, H.L. October 2010. "Don't Tweak Your Supply Chain—Rethink It End to End." *Harvard Business Review* 88, no. 10, pp. 62–69.

Murray, C.J. 2003. "Emerging Markets—'smart' Data Sets." *Electronic Engineering Times* 38.

Narayanan, V.G. and A. Raman. November 2004. "Aligning Incentives in Supply Chains." *Harvard Business Review 82, no. 11,* pp. 94–102.

O'Connell, A. November 2007. "Improve Your Returns on Returns." *Harvard Business Review 85, no. 11,* pp. 30–34.

Prokesch, S. 2010. "The Sustainable Supply Chain." *Harvard Business Review* 88, no. 10, pp. 70–72.

Multiple Choice Questions

1. What are the guidelines that Heinz implemented when they began entering new global markets?

   a. The 5 W's
   b. The 3 L's
   c. The 4 A's
   d. The 3 C's
   e. The 4 H's

2. Which of the following was not emphasized by Heinz when entering emerging markets?

   a. Applicability
   b. Availability
   c. Affinity
   d. Ambiguity
   e. Affordability

3. _____ are/is responsible for developing capabilities and managing performance, which includes measuring, evaluating, and recognizing performance when it comes to customer service.

   a. Facility managers
   b. Human Resources
   c. C-Suite officers
   d. Customers
   e. Marketing

4. Which of the following is not a private sector industry that is purely services?

   a. Cleaning
   b. Hotels
   c. Banking
   d. Insurance
   e. Social services

5. Which of the following is not a factor that impacts customer satisfaction, according to the textbook?

   a. Price
   b. Service quality
   c. Situational factors
   d. Competitive advantage
   e. Personal factors

6. _____ is an accumulation of learned meaning within a human population.

   a. Social environment
   b. Culture
   c. Legal environment
   d. Behavior
   e. Knowledge

7. The _____ is an analytic framework for translating a company's vision and high-level business strategy into specific, quantifiable goals and for monitoring performance against those goals.

   a. Balance scorecard
   b. Pareto analysis
   c. Balance sheet
   d. Income summary
   e. Human Resource department

8. Which of the following is not a service quality dimension mentioned in the text?

   a. Reliability
   b. Responsiveness
   c. Consistency
   d. Assurance
   e. Empathy

9. According to a 2008 study published in the *Journal of Service Research*, what is the most important question you can ask for your business?

   a. "What does the customer need?"
   b. "What is our customer service level?"
   c. "What is our customer satisfaction level?"
   d. "What does the customer want?"
   e. "How can I make this product/service better?"

10. In satisfying the customers' needs, which of the following is not an action to take in measuring and evaluating performance?

    a. Reward high performers
    b. Monitor service behaviors/results
    c. Solicit customer and employee feedback
    d. Keep score
    e. Evaluate performance

11. Which of the following is not one of the 10 common expectations that management should keep in mind with knowing the customer?

    a. Be accessible
    b. Follow-up
    c. Treat customers with courtesy
    d. Provide well-trained and informed employees
    e. Survey the customer

12. Which analysis to service operations can show that in many cases, approximately 80 percent of the turnover (i.e., stock) can be ascribed to approximately 20 percent of the customers, articles, or orders?

    a. Deming analysis
    b. Pareto analysis
    c. Customer analysis
    d. Structured analysis
    e. Ohno analysis

13. Directly relating a financial measure such as _____ with an operations metric like _____ is a new idea at the Dallas-based airline, in the Mini-Case Southwest Airlines Co.

   a. Pareto analysis, forecasting
   b. Cumulative sales, cross-docking
   c. Lower costs, fast ground turnaround
   d. Increase profit, lowering lead times
   e. Gap model, service delivery

14. Which company had to completely forgo its "beef specialty" and instead offered lamb and veggie patties in India?

   a. Burger King
   b. Wendy's
   c. McDonald's
   d. Five Guys
   e. Bojangles

15. Which of the following is not a goal specified on a balanced scorecard example?

   a. Profit margin
   b. Waste reduction
   c. Cash flow
   d. Revenue growth
   e. Return on Assets (ROA)

CHAPTER 11

SCM Trends

Global environment		
The supply chain		**Supply chain flows**
Intercorporate coordination (functional shifting, third-party providers, relationship management, supply chain structures)		*Two-way flows*
Inter-functional coordination trust, commitment, risk, dependence, behaviors	Marketing	
	Sales	Products
	Research and development	Services
	Forecasting	Information
	Production	Financial resources
	Purchasing	
	Logistics	
	Inventory management	
	Information systems	*One-way flows*
	Finance	← Demand
	Customer service	Forecasts →
Supplier's supplier ↔ Supplier ↔ Focal firm ↔ Customer ↔ Customer's customer		

(Customer satisfaction/ value/ profitability/ competitive advantage)

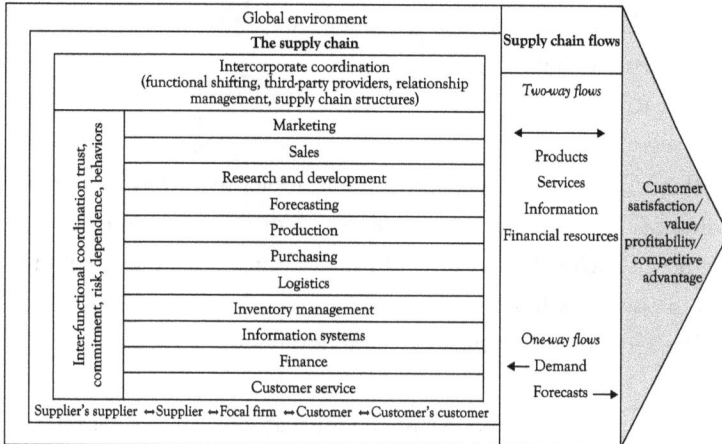

Chapter Objectives

- Assess the continued use of information sharing
- Review the trend from vertical to virtual integration
- Examine the continued growth of reverse logistics
- Present thought-provoking ideas for management

It is important to realize that the current drivers of change in the supply chain will continue to impact the supply chain in the foreseeable future. Just as important is to acknowledge that these processes are simply a part of an ever-changing system. It is not good enough to understand today's issues without addressing the future impacts of these changes, evolving technology, economic issues, and so on. We have addressed some of what we call today's trends earlier, they include:

- Actual customer demand: speed, flexibility and competitive pricing;
- The outsourcing trend will continue to increase;

- New software: ERP, sophisticated application software will continue to be implemented;
- New technologies will continue to be used to supply product information.
    - ○ EDI
    - ○ Internet, intranet, extranet
    - ○ Wireless communications
    - ○ Teleconferencing and telecommuting
    - ○ Bar-coding
    - ○ RFID

These issues are just a continuation of topics that firms are currently addressing. There are other trends, however, that are just beginning to be seen now, which will increase in the near future. Thus, there is always a need to assess new future trends.

One set of trends are the logical implications of the four global forces.

- Integration of extended international activities into a coordinated global system.
- Restructuring the global supply chain network to avoid duplicated processes.
- Global expansion of small- and medium-sized firms.

However, another set of trends comes directly from this increase in global competition. Specifically, there will continue to be an intensification of traffic in global logistics channels. The implications are as follows:

- Straining infrastructure capacity in many areas.
- Every mode of transportation will be affected.
- Effects: Congestion, bottlenecks, longer delivery times, reduced transport reliability.
- Results: Higher costs, diminished effectiveness.

Also, there is one additional trend that European firms have to deal with now, which U.S. firms will eventually have to address. That is the rapid growth of return flows, otherwise known as reverse logistics (RL).

This is caused by environmental awareness (greening of the supply chain), more aggressive sales techniques, and an imbalance between flows at an international level.

Shift From Vertical to Virtual Integration

Henry Ford pushed for vertical integration. In other words, he wished to own the entire value chain required to build a car. His thinking was that by doing this, he could reduce waste and increase efficiency. At its peak, Ford's rubber plantations, steel mills, ships, railroads, and manufacturing facilities could convert raw materials to a car in seven days; however, this required huge amounts of capital and a complex administration. Companies cannot have core competencies that include every aspect of their supply chain. Any process or function of an organization that is not a core competency is one that can cause inefficiency. Additionally, those areas that are not core competencies can be strategically outsourced. Some firms have taken this trend to an extreme where most functions are outsourced.

Outsourcing processes or functions that are not core competencies can relieve the capital requirements of vertical integration while still keeping many of the benefits. Firms that adopt this type of strategy are called virtual companies. Nike is an example of a virtual firm. It consists only of two main sectors: marketing and R&D. Everything else, including logistics, warehousing, manufacturing, and so on, are outsourced. Other firms are following the example of Nike and outsourcing other aspects of their business. In addition to traditionally outsourced functions such as logistics and manufacturing, virtual firms are outsourcing knowledge processes as well. These include functions such as process design and information technology. As firms move to virtual integration, management must realize three important aspects of making the transition:

- First, managers must get used to managing assets, activities, and people they do not control. In many cases in the global environment, managers will never meet the people whose performance they must monitor.

- Second, moving to a virtual organization takes time as partner firms in the supply chain must work to reduce duplication and redundancy.
- Third, management must move beyond interacting with suppliers to working with suppliers' suppliers. These parallel supply chain issues must be addressed when managing the overall organization.

Continued Emphasis on Information Sharing

As more information system technologies are implemented, there will continue to be a greater emphasis on sharing information within members of the supply chain. Increased information sharing allows firms to reduce chaos and uncertainty effects, forecast more accurately, and respond quickly to system changes. The potential cost savings and enhanced services are huge. There are several key issues and trends that impact this implementation goal.

1. Sharing information openly requires a high degree of trust between the firms. This is sometimes limited when in the case of a large firm that requires smaller suppliers to implement technologies for information sharing, which provides the greatest benefits for the larger firm. An example is Walmart requiring all its suppliers to implement EDI in the 1980s and shortly after requiring the implementation of RFID.
2. Some firms will not share forecast or planning data under any circumstances. This limits the type of integration a virtual company might wish for.
3. Desire for shared information is beginning to take novel forms, such as the sharing of employees and cross-functional teams.
4. In some cases, the sharing of information may actually be legally limited. For example, in the Federal Government's view, there is a fine line between sharing information to improve forecasts and fixing prices. Thus, changes in political administrations can have immediate impacts on this trend.

Move From Managerial Accounting to Value-Based Accounting

In the wake of the Enron scandal, firms have become aware of the limitations of generally accepted accounting procedures (GAAP). During the past decade, many firms have moved to managerial accounting practices such as activity-based costing. The benefits of these changes have encouraged firms to look at ways to assess how their work impacts shareholder value. This has led to the adoption of economic value added (EVA) and market value added (MVA) tools. These types of tools lend themselves to being used with the information readily available from ERP systems. This is being driven by the fact that managers are being forced to show how supply chain changes affect the overall health of the firm.

Focus on Security

In the wake of September 11, 2001, security has become a major SCM issue. Railroads, ocean shippers and trucking companies have had to spend large amounts of time and money in efforts to increase the security of cargo and to make sure that cargo is not used for terrorist purposes. The drive for this is both from an ethical requirement and the desire to protect against potential legal ramifications. The requirements for individual supply chain companies remain in flux as federal legal requirements change and as new security technologies are developed. Sadly however, the impact of this particular trend will continue to grow as the world becomes an increasingly dangerous place to conduct business.

Reverse Logistics

RL is a process in which a manufacturer systematically accepts previously shipped products or parts from the point of consumption for possible recycling, remanufacturing, resale, or disposal. Thus, an RL system incorporates a supply chain that has been redesigned to manage the backward flow of products or parts destined for remanufacturing, recycling, resale, or disposal.

The management of RL processes breaks down into two general areas: product returns and product packaging. Product returns are heavily driven by customer returns and vary in volume by industry. Product packaging involves recycling of cardboard, plastic, and other packaging material to reduce disposal costs. Processes involved in RL include collection of used, damaged, unwanted, or outdated products as well as packaging and shipping materials.

RL isn't a new concept, but it is an increasingly important one. "Returns have existed from the first time anyone manufactured a product or opened a store," says Buzzy Wyland, president of manufacturing services with third-party logistics provider (3PL) Genco Distribution. "What's changed—and it was about ten years ago—is that people started to focus on the real costs involved in returns, which evolved into reverse logistics." Those costs become an issue when returns become a problem. "Most companies have never given reverse logistics much focus," says John McVicker, Genco's VP customer start-ups. "Some may be aware that reverse logistics was a problem, but most are focused on the sales end of their business and disregard the returns piece." In order to compare the return demands of various industries, refer to the following table.

Industry	Return Percentage
Magazine Publishing	50%
Book Publishers	20%–30%
Book Distributors	10%–20%
Greeting Cards	20%–30%
Catalog Retailers	18%–35%
Electronic Distributors	10%–12%
Computer Manufacturers	10%–20%
CD-ROMS	18%–25%
Printers	4%–8%
Mail Order Computer Manufacturers	2%–5%
Mass Merchandiser	4%–15%
Consumer Electronics	4%–5%
Household Chemicals	2%–3%
Auto Industry (Parts)	4%–6%

To better conceptualize the business dimension here, consider the auto industry (parts segment) listed last in the table. While that 4 to 6 percent of returns may seem low, 90 to 95 percent of all automobile starters and alternators sold for replacement in the United States are remanufactured. The Auto Parts Remanufacturers Association estimates the market for remanufactured parts to be $36 billion.

So, should you be concerned with RL? On one hand, there are no legal requirements for it in the United States, although there are in Europe. While there are no legal requirements to induce U.S. companies to adopt RL systems, there may be operational reasons. Specifically, there are symptoms in operations that returns have become a problem. According to Dr. Richard Dawe with the Fritz Institute of International Logistics those are as follows:

- Returns arrive faster than processing or disposal.
- Large amounts of return inventory held in the warehouse.
- Unidentified or unauthorized returns.
- Lengthy cycle processing times.
- Unknown total cost of the returns process.
- Customers have lost confidence in the repair activity.

While the symptoms of problem returns can be applied across products and industries, solutions to managing RL are not as general. Unique product dispositions will require different companies to use different RL techniques. However, the goal for everyone's the same: get the highest value possible from returned items.

Types of Reverse Logistics Systems

Designing and developing an RL supply chain is different from forward logistics in several ways. Differences include the supply chain composition and structure (new parties may be involved and new roles assumed by existing parties, and the forward network may be different from the RL network); additional government constraints; rapid timing and uncertainty in the environment.

To date, a great deal of RL network research has been done, mostly in Europe. This research has addressed topics as varied as:

- Recycling steel by-products;
- Sand recycling;

- Electronic equipment collection and remanufacturing;
- Carpet recycling;
- A general model investigating the various effects of environmental variables on return flows.

One of the more prolific researchers in RL is M. Fleischmann. He has proposed a generic RL network model based on a mixed integer linear program and presented a continuous optimization model for RL network design. Most important for our discussion here is that he has devised a framework of three typical RL network structures: RL networks for bulk recycling, remanufacturing, and reuse (Table 11.1). This provides a useful way of viewing RL networks and allows us an overview of the various requirements of different types of systems.

As an example of how to apply this, we will look at carpet recycling. Carpet recycling clearly falls into the bulk recycling category, which is characterized by substantial initial RL investment costs relative to the product value (low-value density), as well as a high vulnerability with respect to uncertainty in the supply volume. The network structure is often flat and centralized at the recycling stage due to the expensive recycling equipment. The system is open loop, meaning that the recycling activities do not interfere with new product sales. Cooperation within the industry often takes place, mainly to ensure input volumes. It is easy to see that carpet recycling closely matches this category, making the volume

Table 11.1 Overview of RL network types (based on Fleischman)

	Bulk Recycling	**Remanufacturing**	**Reuse**
Structure	• Centralized • Flat • Open loop • Branchwide cooperation	• Decentralized • Multilevel • Closed loop • No branch cooperation	• Decentralized • Flat • Closed loop • No branch cooperation
Generation	New reverse networks	Extension of forward networks	Extension of forward networks
Ownership	Third parties, material suppliers, OEMs	Mostly Original Equipment Manufacturers (OEMs)	OEMs, third parties

and variability of recyclable carpet a problem of prime importance. In addition to affecting economics, the uncertainty in the quantity and timing or product returns often leads to increased difficulties in planning for RL as compared to forward logistics.

Global Comparison of Reverse Logistics

As mentioned in the previous section, Europe has laws requiring RL systems for manufacturing. This is due to the fact that in Europe there is a great deal of environmental awareness of the depletion of natural resources. This leads to an awareness of customers for green branding and new markets for returned goods. Another reason is cost minimization. Companies that use RL, coupled with recycling or remanufacturing, have been estimated to save 40 to 60 percent of the cost of manufacturing a completely new product. Finally, European firms are becoming aware that using RL may cut down delivery lead times, for example, if service parts or, more generally, complex components are remanufactured rather than manufactured from scratch. All of this has led to more research and applications in this area. The laws that have been implemented requiring the recycling of many types of goods effectively increase and stabilize return flows of products.

In the United States, the main environmental driver for some industries is the need to reduce the amount of material going into landfills. An example of this is the carpet industry. Increasingly, local governments are looking to reduce landfill use and putting pressure on manufacturers to take steps toward source reduction. In 2000, 5.1 billion pounds of waste carpet were landfilled in the United States, costing over $90 million just in dumping fees. Moreover, federal, state/provincial, and municipal governments in North America have started implementing energy management programs, as part of which they promote the purchase of carpet with at least 25 percent recycled content. As a result, U.S. carpet manufacturers signed a memorandum of agreement in 2002, making it a target to divert 40 percent of carpet waste flow from landfills by 2012. Between 20 and 25 percent of all used carpet will be recycled. This requires the setup of an RL system to handle the collection of used carpet, the separation of carpet components, and the redistribution of recyclable materials to carpet manufacturers. First attempts at this have been made in the sector of commercial carpets, and the willingness exists to sell recycled carpets in the consumer market.

Unlike forward logistics, however, RL operations are complex and prone to a high degree of uncertainty, affecting collection rates, recycling lead times, and capacities in the reverse channel. Part of this uncertainty lies in the fact that the physical distances that RL networks in the United States must cover, are much larger than in Europe with its higher population densities. Thus, U.S. carpet manufacturers and other players in the RL chain are interested in knowing how to best structure their RL systems and what operational difficulties they will have to face.

Focus on Application

RL is practiced in many industries, including those producing steel, commercial aircraft, computers, automobiles, chemicals, appliances, and medical items. Companies that have practiced RL include BMW, Delphi, DuPont, General Motors, Hewlett-Packard, Storage Tek, and TRW. RL is also widely used in the automobile industry. It provides automobile firms with far-reaching cost and strategic advantages in a highly competitive industry. BMW's strategic goal is to design a "totally reclaimable" automobile by the 21st century. Its objective is to recover, recondition, and then reuse all parts. The effective use of RL can help a firm to compete in its industry, especially when confronting intense competition and low profit margins.

Key Takeaways

- Trends reflect continued increases in information sharing, supporting virtual integration and demanding increased support from IT foundations.
- Security is increasing in importance not only for international but also domestic supply chain activities.
- RL continues to increase in importance. Companies that do not address this area will weaken their competitive position in the marketplace as others strengthen themselves in the reverse supply chain.

Reflection Points

1. How can you help steer your company toward the future? What type of future trend analysis do you have in place in your firm? How far into the future do you plan and look for trends—5, 10, or 20 years?

2. In your particular industry, what are the drivers that have limited or supported RL development?

3. Does your organization proactively manage its reverse supply chain? If not, why not? Could optimizing your reverse supply chain give you a strategic advantage over your competition?

4. How has the Covid-19 crisis of 2020 changed your reverse supply chain? Can you process items in the same manner? Do you even accept returns of all your items? Is there a market for items in your industry's reverse supply chain?

5. What are your thoughts on how some e-commerce companies no longer accept returns yet still give a return credit? How do you think that they ultimately pay for this type of concession?

Additional Resources

Donovan, J. 2003. "RF Identification Tags: Show Me the Money." *Electronic Engineering Times* 41.

Elllis, S. and S. Lambright. 2002. "Real Time Tech-Unilever See Intelligent Product Tags as the Brains Behind Real-Time Supply Chains." *Optimize* 44.

Gilligand, M. and D. Prince. 2001. "New Approaches to 'Unforecastable' Demand." *Journal of Business Forecasting Methods and Systems* 20, no. 2, pp. 9–13.

Karkkainen, M. and J. Holmstrom. 2002. "Wireless Product Identification: Enabler for Handling Efficiency, Customisation and Information Sharing." *Supply Chain Management: An International Journal* 7, no. 4, pp. 242–252.

Lee, H.L. October 2010. "Don't Tweak Your Supply Chain-Rethink It End to End." *Harvard Business Review* 88, no. 10, pp. 62–69.

Murray, C.J. 2003. "Emerging Markets-'Smart' Data Sets." *Electronic Engineering Times* 38.

O'Connell, A. November 2007. "Improve Your Returns on Returns." *Harvard Business Review* 85, no. 11, pp. 30–34.

Prokesch, S. 2010. "The Sustainable Supply Chain." *Harvard Business Review* 88, no. 10, pp. 70–72.

Multiple Choice Questions

1. The trend that European firms have to deal with now and that U.S. firms will eventually have to address.

   a. Environmental awareness
   b. Reverse logistics
   c. Globalization
   d. Congestion
   e. Longer delivery times

2. The man who pushed heavily for vertical integration.

   a. Henry Ford
   b. Fleischman
   c. Taichii Ohno
   d. Elon Musk
   e. Jeff Bezos

3. Firms that outsource processes or functions that are not core competencies to relieve the capital requirements of vertical integration while still keeping many of the benefits, are incorporating what type of methodology?

   a. Vertical integration
   b. Bottlenecks
   c. Information sharing
   d. Virtual integration
   e. GAAP

4. What are the only two sectors virtual integration includes and does not outsource?

   a. Marketing, R&D
   b. Logistics, Quality
   c. Warehousing, Quality
   d. Warehousing, R&D
   e. Manufacturing, Marketing

5. Increased _____ allows firms to reduce chaos and uncertainty effects, forecast more accurately, and respond quickly to system changes.

   a. Bottlenecks
   b. Efficiency
   c. Information sharing
   d. Vertical integration
   e. Lead times

6. Sharing information openly requires a high degree of _____ between the firms.

   a. Information
   b. RFID
   c. Trust
   d. Efficiency
   e. Value

7. A reverse logistics system incorporates a supply chain that has been redesigned to manage the backward flow of products or parts destined for all of the following except?

   a. Manufacturing
   b. Recycling
   c. Resale
   d. Disposal
   e. Design

8. The management of RL processes breaks down into two general areas _____ and _____.

   a. Product returns, product packaging
   b. Product design, product returns
   c. Product design, product packaging
   d. Product quality, product configuration
   e. Product configuration, product packaging

9. Specifically, there are symptoms in operations that returns have become a problem. According to Dr. Richard Dawe, those are all of the following except?

    a. Returns arriving faster than processing or disposal
    b. Large amount of returns inventory held in the warehouse
    c. Unidentified or unauthorized returns
    d. Identification of too many bottlenecks
    e. Lengthy cycle processing times

10. What is the goal of everyone in reverse logistics?

    a. Improve efficiency.
    b. Establish better customer service.
    c. Get the highest value possible from returned items.
    d. Prevent from receiving too many returns.
    e. Increase your company's recycling levels.

11. The structure best used for bulk recycling is

    a. Decentralized
    b. Closed loop
    c. Centralized
    d. Multilevel

12. Reuse tends to use a _____ system.

    a. Decentralized
    b. Third party
    c. Network
    d. Linear

13. Symptoms that returns are a problem include, but are not limited to, all of the following except:

    a. Returns arriving faster than processing.
    b. Lengthy cycle times.
    c. Customers have lost confidence in repair activities.
    d. Return costs are increasing.

14. Sharing information openly requires a high degree of _____ between the firms.

    a. Trust
    b. Liability
    c. Confidentiality
    d. Planning

15. Desire for shared information is beginning to take forms such as _____ employees.

    a. Trading
    b. Sharing
    c. Training
    d. Firing

Answers

Chapter 1—Supply Chain Management

1. b	2. c	3. b	4. d	5. b
6. a	7. d	8. d	9. b	10. e
11. c	12. c	13. b	14. d	15. a

Chapter 2—The Global Stage

1. c	2. d	3. e	4. c	5. a
6. b	7. c	8. d	9. d	10. d
11. b	12. a	13. c	14. a	15. b

Chapter 3—Forecasting

1. d	2. c	3. b	4. e	5. b
6. a	7. c	8. d	9. b	10. a
11. c	12. d	13. a	14. c	15. d

Chapter 4 —Inventory Management

1. c	2. b	3. e	4. b	5. d
6. a	7. e	8. a	9. c	10. b
11. d	12. d	13. a	14. b	15. e

Chapter 5—Distribution

1. a	2. c	3. b	4. d	5. c
6. b	7. c	8. a	9. e	10. d
11. a	12. b	13. d	14. a	15. e

Chapter 6—Uncertainty

1. a	2. d	3. c	4. b	5. a
6. e	7. b	8. a	9. c	10. d
11. c	12. d	13. a	14. b	15. c

Chapter 7—Information Technology

1. d	2. b	3. c	4. c	5. e
6. d	7. d	8. c	9. a	10. b
11. a	12. d	13. c	14. d	15. d

Chapter 8—Strategy and the Supply Chain

1. b	2. c	3. a	4. d	5. d
6. b	7. a	8. c	9. a	10. a

Chapter 9—Supplier Selection

1. b	2. c	3. a	4. b	5. d
6. c	7. e	8. d	9. c	10. d
11. a	12. a	13. a	14. a	15. c

Chapter 10—Customer Service

1. c	2. d	3. b	4. e	5. d
6. b	7. a	8. c	9. d	10. a
11. e	12. b	13. c	14. c	15. b

Chapter 11—SCM Trends

1. b	2. a	3. d	4. a	5. c
6. c	7. e	8. a	9. d	10. c
11. c	12. a	13. d	14. a	15. b

Reader's Notes

As you may have noticed while reading the book, many of the readings listed at the end of the chapter were not from the latest journal articles. This was a deliberate choice. This book is intended for mid- to upper-level executives who are NOT supply chain management professionals, but need to have a better understanding of key components of SCM so that they can support their company's competitive issues. As such, it is expected that you will be interacting with the supply chain directors within your company. Most, if not all, of these individuals will have come through the ranks over the course of years. Thus, the authors chose to include articles that have been used by professionals throughout the past several years. The goal is to help you understand how the profession has adapted over time. However, for those of you who wish to look at current issues, now and in the future, we suggest the following:

Organizations

CSCMP: Council of Supply Chain Management Professionals. (http://cscmp. org/) Formerly the Council of Logistics Management (CLM), they refer to themselves as the world's leading source for the supply chain management profession. They provide excellent conferences and published materials on various SCM topics.

ISM: Institute for Supply Management (www.ism.ws/). This is another key SCM group that also focuses on purchasing. Many nonSCM executives are familiar with ISM due to their manufacturing reports that are used as economic indicators.

Researchers

Dr. Martin Christopher, SCM Researcher, Cranfield University. Dr. Christopher has published books and articles on logistics, SCM, and relationship marketing. Of potential use to many executives is the fact that they have been translated into most of the major languages worldwide.

Dr. Hau Lee, SCM Researcher, Stanford University. While some of his articles are primarily for researchers, many of his Harvard Business Reviews articles provide keen insights in SCM issues.

Dr. John T. (Tom) Mentzer, University of Tennessee. Although recently deceased, Dr. Mentzer wrote over 8 books and 190 articles during his career. He was the most prolific author in the *Journal of Business Logistics*, which provide articles that executives will find readable and informative.

Dr. David Simchi-Levi, SCM Researcher, MIT. While many of his articles are heavily mathematical, they provide useful insights into designing SCM networks. His supply chain textbook is used throughout the country.

References

Birdyback. n.d. Monash Business School. www.monashedu/business/marketing/marketing-dictionary/b/birdyback (accessed April 8, 2021).

Chopra, S. and P. Meindl. 2004. *Supply Chain Management: Strategy, Planning and Operation,* 2nd ed. Upper Saddle River, NJ: Pearson.

Courtney, H., J. Kirkland, and P. Viguerie. 1997. "Strategy Under Uncertainty." *Harvard Business Review 75, no. 6, pp. 67–82.*

Fishyback. n.d. Monash Business School. www.monashedu/business/marketing/marketing-dictionary/f/fishyback (accessed April 8, 2021).

Forrester. 1961. Industrial Dynamics. Cambridge, MA: MIT Press.

Jones, M.P. 1990. "An Investigation Into the Logistical Performance of a Partially Just-in-Time Supply Chain by the Application of Discrete Event Simulation." *Thesis.* University of Warwick.

Kim, B. and H. Oh. 2000. "An Exploratory Inquiry Into the Perceived Effectiveness of a Global Information System." *Information Management and Computer Security 8,* no. 3, pp. 144–153.

Lee, H.L. and S. Whang. 1998. Information Sharing in a Supply Chain. Stanford, Graduate School of Business, Stanford University.

Lee, H.L., V. Padmanabhan, and S. Whang. 1997. "Information Distortion in a Supply Chain: The Bullwhip Effect." Management Science 43, no. 4, pp. 546–558.

Maloni, M.J. and W.C. Benton. 1997. "Supply Chain Partnerships: Opportunities for Operations Research." *European Journal of Operational Research* 101, no. 3, pp. 419–429.

Mintzberg, H. 1994. "Rethinking Strategic Planning Part I: Pitfalls and Fallacies." Long Range Planning 27, pp. 12–21.

Newman, S. and R. Ford. 2021. "Five Steps to Leading Your Team in the Virtual COVID-19 Workplace." *Organizational Dynamics 50,* no. 1. https://doi.org/10.1016/j.orgdyn.2020.100802.

Porter, M. 1980. *Competitive Advantage.* New York, NY: Free Press.

Pranggono, B. and A. Arabo. 2020. "COVID-19 Pandemic Cybersecurity Issues." Internet *Technology Letters 4,* no. 2. https://doi.org/10.1002/itl2.247.

Taylor, D.H. 2000. "Demand Amplification: Has It Got Us Beat?" International Journal of Physical Distribution and Logistics Management 30, no. 6, pp. 515–533.

Wilding, R.D. 1998. "The Supply Chain Complexity Triangle: Uncertainty Generation in the Supply Chain." International Journal of Physical Distribution and Logistics Management 28, no. 8, pp. 599–616.

Wilding, R.D. and J.F. Hill. 1999. "Parallel Interactions in Supply Chains." In 2nd International Symposium on Advanced Manufacturing Processes, Systems and Technologies. AMPST 99.

About the Authors

Dr. Edmund Prater teaches Global Operations and Logistics at the University of Texas at Arlington. He received his PhD, MSIE, and MSEE from the Georgia Institute of Technology. He became interested in global supply chains when he started and ran an import/export firm in Russia in the early 1990s. Most recently, he completed a fellowship with the National Academy of Sciences. As a Jefferson Science Fellow, he worked at the U.S. State Department in the Bureau of Educational and Cultural Affairs. His work has been published in journals including *The Journal of Operations Management, The International Journal of Operations and Production Management, Communications of the ACM, The International Journal of Physical Distribution and Logistics Management, Medical Group Management, The International Journal of Health Systems and Informatics, and Decision Sciences Journal of Innovative Education*. Besides his academic career, he was in charge of AI Development as a senior manager in BellSouth's Technology Assessment Group. Dr. Prater has received research grants from the Small Business Administration as well as the French Government.

Kim Whitehead is currently an associate professor of quantitative management at Anderson University in Anderson, South Carolina. She received her PhD in management science from the University of Texas at Arlington, her MBA in management from Florida State University, and a BBA in accounting from Georgia College and State University. At Anderson University she created successful undergraduate and graduate programs specializing in supply chain management. Prior to teaching, she spent over 20 years in the consumer products industry where she served in multiple financial capacities. Her career focus has been on bridging the roles of finance and operations in manufacturing environments. Most recently, she served as the chief financial officer for a worldwide manufacturer and distributor of branded consumer products.

Index

Letters '*f*' and '*t*' after locators indicate figures and tables, respectively.

OTHER TITLES IN THE SUPPLY AND OPERATIONS MANAGEMENT COLLECTION

Joy M. Field, Boston College, Editor

- *Process Improvement to Company Enrichment* by Daniel Plung and Connie Krull
- *Organizational Velocity* by Alan Amling
- *C-O-S-T* by Craig Theisen
- *RFID for the Supply Chain and Operations Professional, Third Edition* by Pamela J. Zelbst and Victor Sower
- *Operations Management in China, Second Edition* by Craig Seidelson
- *Futureproofing Procurement* by Katie Jarvis-Grove
- *How Efficiency Changes the Game* by Ray Hodge
- *Supply Chain Planning, Second Edition* by Matthew J. Liberatore and Tan Miller
- *Sustainable Quality* by Joseph Diele
- *Why Quality is Important and How It Applies in Diverse Business and Social Environments, Volume II* by Paul Hayes
- *Why Quality is Important and How It Applies in Diverse Business and Social Environments, Volume I* by Paul Hayes
- *The Cost* by Chris Domanski

Concise and Applied Business Books

The Collection listed above is one of 30 business subject collections that Business Expert Press has grown to make BEP a premiere publisher of print and digital books. Our concise and applied books are for...

- Professionals and Practitioners
- Faculty who adopt our books for courses
- Librarians who know that BEP's Digital Libraries are a unique way to offer students ebooks to download, not restricted with any digital rights management
- Executive Training Course Leaders
- Business Seminar Organizers

Business Expert Press books are for anyone who needs to dig deeper on business ideas, goals, and solutions to everyday problems. Whether one print book, one ebook, or buying a digital library of 110 ebooks, we remain the affordable and smart way to be business smart. For more information, please visit www.businessexpertpress.com, or contact sales@businessexpertpress.com.

www.ingramcontent.com/pod-product-compliance
Lightning Source LLC
Chambersburg PA
CBHW061209220326
41599CB00025B/4580